南無本師釋迦牟尼佛
Namo Root Guru Shakyamuni Buddha

法　海　譯　叢

THE MAJOR BUDDHIST CANON

(2)

Vairocana Publishing Company, Ltd.
毘盧出版社　敬印

The Major Buddhist Canon (2)

金剛般若波羅蜜經
The Diamond Prajna-Paramita Sutra
(*The Diamond Sutra*)

An Annotated Edition with Chinese Text
Second Edition
英漢合訂本・第二版

Translated and Annotated by
Ven. Cheng Kuan
53rd Generation Acharya of Shingon Sect
高野山眞言宗五十三世阿闍梨
釋成觀法師英譯

Americana Buddhist Temple, USA
Mahavairochana Temple, Taiwan
美國遍照寺・台灣大毘盧寺 發行

The Diamond Prajna-Paramita Sutra

2nd. Edition 2007

First Edition, Copyright © 2005 (on Buddha's Joyous Day) by Vairocana Publishing Co., Ltd.
All Rights Reserved (**For free distribution only**)
Printed in Taipei, Taiwan

Distributing Centers:

Mahavairochana Temple

No.15, Alley 6, Lane 4, Fu-Hsing Rd., Wenshan District, Taipei City 11691, Taiwan
Ph.: (02) 2934-7281 Fax: (02) 2930-1919
Website: www.abtemple.org

Americana Buddhist Temple

10515 N. Latson Rd., Howell, MI 48855, USA
Ph.: (517) 545-7559 Fax: (517) 545-7558
Website: www.abtemple.org

ISBN 957-9373-20-5

Contents

The Diamond Prajna-Paramita Sutra

金剛般若波羅蜜經（漢譯本）
The Chinese Text of the Sutra

Appendix
附　錄

Foreword for
The Initial Three Sutras' Publication
of *The Major Buddhist Canon*

It has always been my greatest wish to translate the Right Buddha Dharma and make it available for all people in the world, so as to benefit infinite Multi-beings globally; and now I have finished translating several Sutras into English, which I entitle as *The Major Buddhist Canon*. Among these, three of them— *The Sutra of Forty-two Chapters, The Diamond Sutra*, and *The Altar-Sutra of the Sixth Patriarch*—are done with page layout using PageMaker, and so are ready for publishing. And I plan to have several thousand copies of each of them printed this time, so that we may send them as free gifts to the libraries of the capital cities of all the countries, of all the major cities, and major universities around the world. Therefore, I wish that all good believers of the Dharma could be aspired to get involved in this supreme enterprise of the *Thus-Adventist's Dharmic Corpus* by making a donation towards the publication, so as to help infinite Sentient-kinds plant the *Virtuous Roots* for the Supreme Enlightenment.

Moreover, the three Sutras that are being published are each of them in their own way, the "First Sutra." Here are the reasons:

(1) ***The Sutra of Forty-two Chapters***—This Sutra was brought to China in the Eastern Han Dynasty (1ˢᵗ Century A.D.) on the back of a white horse, and was the first Sutra ever translated into Chinese. Hence this Sutra is deemed as "the First Sutra" in this way, and has become a very significant Sutra for this reason. And now because this Sutra is also the first one in The English version to be published, its symbolic meaning is beyond expression.

(2) ***The Diamond Sutra***—This Sutra is one of the most important portion in the whole 600 Books of *The Great Prajna-Paramita Sutra,* and so in this way it stands as the "First Sutra" in the Dharma. Furthermore,

starting from the Sixth Patriarch of Ch'an Sect, this Sutra has been traditionally utilized as the chief resorting basis for *"Mind-Verification"* by both patriarchs and general Ch'an practitioners; hence it is also deemed as the First Sutra by this virtue.

(3) ***The Altar-Sutra of the Sixth Patriarch***—It has been well acknowledged that the greatest contribution that Chinese Buddhism has ever made to the world is the achievement of the Ch'an teachings. Yet it was all due to the extraordinary Merits and good *Karmic Occasions* of the Sixth Patriarch that made the flourish of Ch'an in China possible. For this reason, *the Altar-Sutra of the Sixth Patriarch*, along with *the Diamond Sutra*, has become the two predominant Scriptures in the teachings of Ch'an lineage in the wake of the Sixth Patriarch. (Since Song Dynasty though, the third Scripture, *the Chronicle of Lamp-Transmission*, has been added to the Ch'anist's practicing syllabus.) In consequence, this Sutra, besides *the Diamond Sutra,* is virtually the "First Sutra" for the learning and practice of Mahayana Ch'an.

Due to the fact that the aforesaid three Sutras are all the topmost Sutras in their own virtues, the Meritorious Virtues acquired through the involvement in helping them circulated and propagated are incredibly great.

Furthermore, according to *The Sutra of Upasaka-Precept,* the Merits in the Dharmic Bestowal of printing Sutras are highly superior. Part of the Text from this Sutra is cited below for the reference of good believers, and for them to practice in compliance with the Holy Teachings:

Good virtuous man, there are two kinds of *Bestowals*: first, *Dharmic Bestowal*; second, *Monetary Bestowal.* The *Retributions* acquired by *Dharmic Bestowal* can include the *Retribution of Property* and the *Retribution of Dharma.* Yet *Monetary Bestowal* only result in the *Retribution of Property*....Therefore, *Monetary Bestowal* is inferior, while *Dharmic Bestowal* is superior.

How should one make *Dharmic Bestowal*?
If a *Bhiksu*, or a *Bhiksuni*, or a *Upasaka*, or a
Upasika, is able to instruct others to make them
be endowed with Faith, Precept, Bestowal,
Learning, and Wisdom, either by means of
making others write down the Sutra of the
Buddha's Right Dharma, or by writing it down
themselves; and afterwards they make donations with these written Scriptures to others so
that they may read or incant—this is called
Dharmic Bestowal. Anyone who can make
such *Bestowal* will be able to acquire superior
handsome looks in the infinite future lives.
Wherefore is it so? For the *Multibeings* who
read or hear of the Dharma written will be
able to abolish their mind of Resentment, for
this reason the Donor will be able to obtain
superior handsome looks in the infinite future
lives.

The *Multibeings* who read or hear of the
Dharma written will be able to abolish killing

due to compassion; for this reason the Donor will be able to acquire longevity in the infinite future lives.

The *Multibeings* who read or hear of the Dharma written will be able to refrain from stealing others' property; for this reason the Donor will be able to enjoy copious riches and treasure.

The *Multibeings* who read or hear of the Dharma written will be able to make Bestowals to others with an open mind; for this reason the Donor will be able to obtain great physical strength in the infinite future lives.

The *Multibeings* who read or hear of the Dharma written will be able to abolish Self-indulgence; for this reason the Donor will be able to obtain physical ease and felicity in the infinite future lives.

The *Multibeings* who read or hear of the Dharma written will be able to exterminate the mind of *Inanity*; for this reason the Donor will be able to acquire *Unimpeded Eloquence* in the infinite future lives.

The *Multibeings* who read or hear of the Dharma written will be able to engender Faith without any doubts; for this reason the Donor will be able to acquire Faith and Perspicuity in the Mind. And in the like manner he will be able to acquire Precept, Bestowal, Learning, and Wisdom, as well. (—from Segment 19 of *The Sutra of Upasaka Precept*.)

Cheng Kuan
2/19/2005

佛語諦實
決定不虛

—金剛法寶讚

The Words of Buddha are ever truthful without fail.

—Vajraic Maxim

The Diamond
Prajna-Paramita Sutra
(*The Diamond Sutra*)

Namo Root Guru Shakyamuni Buddha.

(Recite three times,
with your palms joined.)

The Sutra-opening Gatha

The supremely profound, wondrously sophisticated
    Dharma
Is hard to encounter in millions of Kalpas.
And now that I am able to hear, read, and uphold it,
I wish to comprehend the real import of the
    Thus-Adventist.

The Diamond[1] Prajna[2]-Paramita[3] Sutra[4]
(*The Diamond Sutra*)

Translated from Sanskrit into Chinese by The Venerable Tri-canon Dharma-master Kumarajiva[5] in the Dynasty of Yao-Chin (344-413 A.D.)

Translated from Chinese into English by Venerable Cheng Kuan, 53rd Generation Acharya of Shingon Sect (1947-)

Segment 1

Thus have I heard: at one time the Buddha sojourned at Jetvana Park in Shravasti State together

---

1. **Diamond**: the hardest material in the world, symbolizing the Transcendental Wisdom that can break all the bad Karmas and impediments while the diamond itself will not break.
2. **Prajna**: Transcendental Wisdom taught by the Buddha which can cure the *Three Venoms* (Avarice, Detestation, and Inanity), so as to attain the Supreme Enlightenment. This Wisdom is totally different from the worldly intelligence or cleverness which can do nothing about reducing bad Karmas or the Three Venoms. *Prajna* is also an *Ultra-mundane Wisdom*, as opposed to the *Mundane Wisdom* (Worldly Wisdom).
3. **Paramita**: Sanskrit, "to the Other Shore." This means metaphorically that by means of Buddha's Transcendental Wisdom, all people (or beings) can *traverse the River of Annoyances and Afflictions* to "the Other Shore" of Nirvana or Enlightenment.
4. **Sutra**: Sanskrit, Holy Scripture.
5. **Kumarajiva**: 344-413 A.D.

3

with an Order of twelve hundred and fifty *Grand Bhiksus*.[6] At that time the *World-Venerated One*,[7] before meal time, putting on His *Cassock* and holding an *Alms Bowl*, entered into the city of Shravasti to seek Alms of food. After having begged in accordance with the *Sequential Begging Rule* in the town, He returned to His domicile. Having taken the meal, put away the *Cassock* and *Bowl* and laved His own feet, the Buddha then arranged the meditation mat, and sat in meditation.

Segment 2

At this time Elder Venerable Subhuti[1] arose amongst the Assembly, bared his right shoulder,[2]

---

6. **Grand Bhiksus**: *Bhiksu*, an ordained Buddhist monk. *Grand Bhiksus*, referring exclusively to Arhats, the Hinayanaist Saints of the highest status.
7. **World-Venerated One**: Sanskrit: *Bhagavam*. One of the Ten Holy Epithets of the Buddha, meaning: one who is venerated by all the worlds, or worshipped universally.
1. **Subhuti**: one of the Ten Great Disciples of the Buddha, renowned for his Wisdom in Comprehending the tenet of *Vacuity*.
2. **bared his right shoulder**: an ancient etiquette in India showing high respect to elders or superiors.

knelt with the right knee on the floor, joined his palms reverently and said to the Buddha: "Your *World-Veneratedship*, it is such a precious rarity that the *Thus-Adventist*[3] has been so very well mindfully protecting the *Pusas*,[4] and have been very well entrusting and instructing the *Pusas*. Your *World-Veneratedship*, for the virtuous men and virtuous women who have already generated the *Anuttara-samyak-sambodhi Heart*,[5] how should they *reside*? And how should they *subjugate* their *Minds*?"

The Buddha said, "Very well said, very well said, Subhuti, just as you have said that the *Thus-Adventist* has been very well mindfully

3. **Thus-Adventist**: Sanskrit: *Tathagata*. Also one of the Ten Holy Epithets of the Buddha, meaning: the "Thus-Comer," or "thus-come one," in some other translations. "Thus," in the manner of the Truthful Way as well as of the Sentient-kind's Karmic Occasions. "Comer," one (the Buddha) who manifests himself in this afflicted world (<u>Advent</u>) to salvage the Multibeings, due to compassion.
4. **Pusa**: the Chinese version for the Sanskrit *Bodhisattva*, meaning: one who seeks the fulfillment of Bodhi, or Enlightenment; next in rank to Buddha among all practitioners.
5. **Anuttara-samyak-sambodhi Heart**: Sanskrit, meaning the "Heart for the Supreme Right Equitable Enlightenment." "Heart," here means Aspiration. This phrase can also be abbreviated as: the *Great Bodhi Heart*.

protecting the *Pusas* and very well entrusting and instructing the *Pusas*. Now listen attentively, and I will expound it for you. The virtuous men and virtuous women who have already generated the *Anuttara-samyak-sambodhi Heart* should *reside* in this wise and should subjugate their minds in this wise :"

"Yes, Your *World-Veneratedship*, we would like very much to hear Your Holiness's instructions."

Segment 3

The Buddha told Subhuti, "The *Pusa Mahasattvas*[1] should thus *subjugate* their own minds: all the genuses of *Multibeings*,[2] such as the *Egg-begotten*, the *Womb-begotten*, the *Moisture-*

---

1. ***Pusa Mahasattvas***: i.e., great Bodhisattvas. *Maha* means great in Sanskrit.
2. ***Multibeings***: the Multitudes. Yet this term includes not just people (mankind), but also the Beings in five other Realms; viz., the Celestial, Asura, Starving Ghost, Purgatory and Animals. Together with Humanity, they are called the Six Realms which constitute the Realm of Transmigration or *Samsara* (Reincarnation).

begotten, or the *Transformation-begotten*,[3] the *Material* or *Immaterial Beings*, the *Conceiving* or *Nonconceiving Beings*, the *Unconceiving* or *Non-unconceiving Beings*[4]—all and sundry of these Beings, I will salvage by delivering them into the *Unremnant Nirvana*.[5] After having thus salvaged infinite, myriad, innumerable Multibeings, in reality there are no Multibeings that have ever been salvaged. Why is it so? Subhuti, for if the *Pusa* fosters the *Ego-appearance*, or the *Alter-appearance*, or the *Multibeing-appearance*, or the *Lifespan-appearance*,[6] he would not be entitled to a *Pusa* in truth."

---

3. *the Egg-begotten…Transformation-begotten*: Collectively these are called the *Four Nativities*.
4. the *Material…or Non-unconceiving Beings*: These are the Celestial Beings of various levels, that have attained various stages of Stasis (*Samadhi*) in their previous lives, and were born in those Heavens according to their level of achievements in Stasis as a Retributional Desert.
5. *Unremnant Nirvana*: the *Nirvana* as attained by Buddhas and *Pusas*, which is consummate, leaving no Impurified Habitudes of Annoyances, as opposed to the *Remnant Nirvana* of Arhats or general Hinayanaists.
6. *Ego-appearance…Lifespan-appearance*: These are the so-called *Quadruple Appearances*, the fundamental Attachments which would stand in one's way to Wisdom, Nirvana, and Enlightenment.

Segment 4

[4-1]

"Furthermore," quoth the Buddha, "Subhuti, as concerns Dharma, a *Pusa* should not *dwell*[1] in any way while practicing *Bestowal*.[2] This would mean that he should not reside in *Matter* while *bestowing*,[3] nor should he *reside* in *Sound*, *Smell*, *Taste*, *Tactile or Dharma* while *bestowing*. Subhuti, a *Pusa* should thus bestow without *dwelling* on any *Appearances*. Wherefore is it so? If a *Pusa* bestows without *dwelling* on *Appearances*, his *Blissful Virtues* would be inconceivable and

---

1. *dwell*: same as "*reside*," a very crucial key word in this *Sutra*, as well as in all the Buddhist practice, especially in Ch'an (or Zen) Buddhism. It means the Attachment or Tenacity in possessing and holding onto something, especially in showing the *indolence* to "move on." This is exactly the sentiment that we would hold with respect to the "house" we *dwell* in (both the material house and the "corporeal house," i.e., the physical body), which we would cling steadfast to, grow attached to, and would not let go of easily, not even when the "lease" is expired.
2. *Bestowal*: Donation, as the first item of the *Six Deliverances* (Six Paramitas), it is one of the most important practices for a *Pusa*, or Mahayanaic Practitioners in general, for it signifies the will to benefit other people, the very central animus of Mahayanaic Altruism.
3. **should not reside in *Matter* while *bestowing***: i.e., not to be attached to Matter, etc., while bestowing.

immeasurable."

[4-2]

"Subhuti," quoth the Buddha, "what do you make of the *Ethereal Space*[4] in the East? Is it conceivable and measurable?"

Subhuti replied, "No, Your *World-Veneratedship*."

"Subhuti," asked the Buddha, "the *Ethereal Spaces* in the South, West, and North, as well as in the *Four Diagonal Directions*,[5] and in the *Zenith* and *Nadir*[6]—would they be conceivable and measurable?"

Subhuti replied, "No, Your *World-Veneratedship*, they are not."

"Subhuti," quoth the Buddha, "if a *Pusa* could perform *Bestowal* without *residing* in *Appearances*, the *Blissful Virtues* that he has acquired

---

4. *Ethereal Space*: i.e., the sky.
5. the *Four Diagonal Directions*: i.e., Northeast, Southeast, Northwest, and Southwest.
6. the *Zenith* and *Nadir*: i.e., up and down (top and bottom).

would be inconceivable and immeasurable in the like way. Subhuti, what a *Pusa* needs to do is nothing but to *reside* according to how he is instructed."[7]

Segment 5

"Subhuti, what would you say to this: could one perceive the *Thus-Adventist* by means of His *Physical Appearances*?"

Subhuti replied, "No, Your *World-Veneratedship*, one could not perceive the *Thus-Adventist* by His *Physical Appearances*. Why is it so? For the *Physical Appearances* that the *Thus-Adventist* has talked about are no *Physical Appearances* at all."

The Buddha told Subhuti, "In fact, all the *Appearances* are *vain* and *delusive*; if one could

7. **to *reside* according to how he is instructed**: i.e., to practice and live one's life by following the Buddha's teachings.

perceive that all *Appearances* are actually *Non-appearances*, one would be perceiving the *Thus-Adventist*."

Segment 6

Subhuti asked the Buddha, "Your *World-Veneratedship*, are there any Multibeings who after hearing such Edicts of *Sutra*[1] are able to engender true Belief?"[2]

The Buddha told Subhuti, "Do not ever say such words; for after the *Thus-Adventist* has gone into *Surcease*,[3] even in the *Last Cycle* of five hundred years,[4] there will still be people who *observe Precepts* and *cultivate Weals* are able to engender

1. *Sutra*: i.e., Buddhist Holy Scripture.
2. **are there...true Belief**: The reason why Subhuti asked this question is because the Tenet of this *Sutra* is so profound that Subhuti is apprehensive that there will not be anyone or few to comprehend and believe in it.
3. **gone into *Surcease***: i.e., gone into *Nirvana*. *Nirvana*, Sanskrit, termination, meaning the termination of all Annoyances and Transmigrations.
4. **the *Last Cycle* of five hundred years**: According to the *Sutras*, there are five cycles of 500 years, totally 2500 years, during which time Buddhism flourishes and declines gradually.

Belief in these Words, even to the extent of recognizing them as truthful.

"In this case, you should know that such people have already cultivated their own *Virtuous Roots*[5] under the Teachings of not just one Buddha, two Buddhas, or three, four, five Buddhas; but in fact, they have already cultivated their own Virtuous Roots at the places of myriads of thousands of Buddhas, so that on hearing these Words again in this lifetime, they would be able to engender *Purified Belief*[6] even within a twinkling of time. Subhuti, the *Thus-Adventist* knows and perceives all about these *Multibeings* that all of them are to acquire such boundless *Weals and Virtues*. Why is it so? For all of these *Multibeings* have already been freed from *Ego-appearance*,[7] *Alter-*

---

5. ***Virtuous Roots***: There are *Five Virtuous Roots*: Faith Root, Diligence Root, Deliberation Root, Stasis Root, and Wisdom Root. They are called "roots," because all the Virtues are engendered out of these fundamental Good Roots, just as the life of a plant depends on its roots for nourishment and stability.

6. ***Purified Belief***: i.e., unadulterated faith, which is not contaminated by skepticism, self-interest, or other unnamed motives.

7. ***Ego-appearance***: i.e., Egoistic Views.

appearance,[8] *Multibeing-appearance*[9] and
Lifespan-appearance;[10] they are also freed from
Dharmic Appearances[11] as well as *Mis-dharmic
Appearances.*[12] Why is it so? For if these *Multi-
beings* seize *Appearances* in the mind, they
would assuredly grow attached to the *Ego, Alter,
Multibeing and Lifespan.* Likewise, if they seize
the *Dharmic Appearances*, they would also be
attached to *Ego, Alter, Multibeing and Lifespan.*
Why is it so?

"For, on the other hand, if they seize the *Mis-
dharmic Appearances*, they are to be attached to
Ego, Alter, Multibeing, and *Lifespan.* Therefore,
one should not seize the *Dharmas*, nor should
one seize the *Mis-dharmas.* By this token, the

8. *Alter-appearance*: i.e., the Views about other persons individually (singular
   number) from the self-centered standpoint.
9. *Multibeing-appearance*: i.e., the View about other people conceived collectively (plural number) from the subjective self-centered standpoint.
10. *Lifespan-appearance*: i.e., the Attachment to life or longevity, as con-
    cerns oneself, others, or all Beings in general.
11. *Dharmic Appearance*: This refers to Attachment to the Buddhist Doc-
    trines.
12. *Mis-dharmic Appearance*: This denotes the theories and practices con-
    trary to Buddha's Teachings, and as such they are both fallacious and
    misleading.

Thus-Adventist is wont to divulge thus: you *Bhiksus*[13] should comprehend that the Dharmas that I have divulged are to be likened to the Analogue of a *Raft*, and it should be noted that even the *Dharmas* are to be abnegated, let alone the *Mis-dharmas*."

Segment 7

"Subhuti," quoth the Buddha, "what do you make of this: does the *Thus-Adventist* obtain *Anuttara-samyak-sambodhi*? Also, does the *Thus-Adventist* have Dharmas to divulge?"

Subhuti replied, "If I understand correctly the imports that the Buddha has imparted, it could be put in this way: there is no *definitive* Dharma, and such is the state named *Anuttara-samyak-sambodhi*; and there is neither *definitive* Dharma that the *Thus-Adventist* divulges. Why is it so?

---

13. **Bhiksu**: an ordained Buddhist monk.

All the Dharmas that the *Thus-Adventist* has divulged are equally unseizable, ineffable, *non-dharmic*, *un-nondharmic*. Why is it so? All the sages and saints can be hierarchized on the basis of the *Dharmas of Non-implementation*."[1]

Segment 8

"Subhuti," quoth the Buddha, "what do you make of this: if someone possesses seven kinds of jewels which are as plenteous as to be able to abound all over the *Three Thousand Mega-thousand Worlds*,[1] and if he employs these riches to bestow on others, would the *Blissful Virtues*

1. **Dharmas of Non-implementation**: i.e., the *Ultra-mundane Dharmas*, or the Dharmas that can lead to Ultimate Liberation. "*Implementation*" means all kinds of illusory employments or undertakings of the worldly people.
1. **Three Thousand Mega-thousand Worlds**: i.e. a *Buddhaic World*, consisting of 100 billion solar systems. This would include: a) One Mini-thousand Cosmoses (i.e., a universe, consisting of 1000 solar systems); b) One Medi-thousand Cosmoses (consisting of 1000 Mini-thousand Cosmoses); c) One Mega-thousand Cosmoses (consisting of 1000 Medi-thousand Cosmoses). Hence, altogether they are called the *Three Thousand Mega-thousand Worlds*. ("World," meaning one solar system, not just the planet Earth.)

thus acquired by this man be plenteous?"

Subhuti replied, "Very much so, Your *World-Veneratedship*. Why is it so? For this *Blissful Virtue* is not the *Essence* of *Blissful Virtue*; therefore, the *Thus-Adventist* divulges that those *Blissful Virtues* are plenteous."

"However," quoth the Buddha, "if there is yet another person who assimilates and upholds the Words in this *Sutra* even as meager as a mere quatrain of *Gatha*,[2] which he relates to other people; the *Blissful Virtues* that this person acquires will be superior to that of the former person. Why is it so? Subhuti, it is due to the fact that all the Buddhas themselves as well as all the *Buddhaic Dharmas* for *Anuttara-samyak-sambodhi* emerge from this *Sutra*. Subhuti, the so-called *Buddhaic Dharmas* are *Non-buddhaic Dharmas*; thus it is denominated as *Buddhaic Dharmas*."

---

2. **Gatha**: Sanskrit, a verse of four-line stanzas (quatrain), usually rhymed in the original Text.

Segment 9

[9-1]

"Subhuti," quoth the Buddha, "what do you make of this: could a *Srota-apanna*[1] make such an *Ideation* as 'I have obtained the *Consummation* of *Srota-apannahood*'?"

Subhuti replied, "No, Your *World-Veneratedship*. Why is it so?   For a *Srota-apanna* signifies '*Stream Entrance*'; yet in reality he never enters anywhere; for he never enters into either *Color*, *Sound*, *Smell*, *Taste*, *Tactile*, or *Dharma*; in consequence, he is entitled to the appellation of *Srota-apanna*."

"Subhuti," quoth the Buddha, "what do you make of this: could a *Sakradagamin*[2] make such an

---

1. *Srota-apanna*: Sanskrit, meaning "entering into Stream (of sainthood)." This is the first Fruition (or Consummation) of Hinayanaic Sainthood. The *First Fruitioner* can attain Arhathood and realize Nirvana after seven reincarnations (seven rebirths) in this world.
2. *Sakradagamin*: the Second Consummation of Hinayanaic Sainthood.   A *Second Fruitioner* will be able to attain Nirvana after one lifetime in the heaven and one rebirth (reincarnation) in this world.

Ideation as 'I have obtained the *Consummation of Sakradagamihood*'?"

Subhuti replied, "No, Your *World-Veneratedship*. Why is it so? For a *Sakradagamin* signifies '*One Coming-and-Going*.' Yet in reality, he never comes or goes; therefore, he is entitled to the appellation of *Sakradagamin*."

"Subhuti," quoth the Buddha, "what do you make of this: could an *Anagamin*[3] make such an Ideation as 'I have obtained the *Consummation of Anagamihood*'?"

Subhuti replied, "No, Your *World-Veneratedship*. Why is it so? For an *Anagamin* signifies '*No Returning*'; yet in reality, there is no *Unreturning*; consequently, he is entitled to the appellation of *Anagamin*."

---

3. *Anagamin*: the Third Consummation of Hinayanaic Sainthood. The *Third Fruitioner* will no longer come back to this world to be reborn. Hence this will be his Final Lifetime in this world; and at the end of this life, he will be born in the Akanistha Heaven, the topmost heaven in the *Matterful Domain*, where he will realize Arhathood and attain Nirvana.

[9-2]

"Subhuti," quoth the Buddha, "what do you make of this: could an *Arhat* make such an *Ideation* as 'I have obtained the *Consummation* of *Arhat Way*'?"[4]

Subhuti replied, "No, Your *World-Veneratedship*. Why is it so? For in reality there is no such Dharma as *Arhathood*. Your *World-Veneratedship*, if ever an *Arhat* should make such an *Ideation* as 'I have obtained the *Arhathood*,' he would still be attached to *Ego, Alter, Multibeing and Lifespan*. Your *World-Veneratedship*, the Buddha has pronounced that I have attained the *Noncontention Samadhi*,[5] which is the first and foremost status ever acquired by any person. Hence I have become the supreme *abstemious*[6]

---

4. the *Consummation* of *Arhat Way*: the Fourth Consummation of Hinayanaic Sainthood.
5. *Noncontention Samadhi*: the state of Stasis (tranquility) plus Prajna (Transcendental Wisdom). "*Noncontention*" means the state free from all annoyances and strifes (*Contentions*). Hence the *Noncontention Samadhi* is a highly prestigious form of Samadhi, attained only by very few great Disciples of the Buddha's.
6. *abstemious*: able to abstain or refrain from, or be liberated from Desires (specif., the Five Desires: the Desires for Wealth, Sex, Fame, Food, and Sleep).

Arhat. Nevertheless, I would never make such an *Ideation* as 'I am an *Abstemious Arhat.*' Your *World-Veneratedship*, if ever I should make such an *Ideation* as 'I have obtained Arhathood,' Your *World-Veneratedship* would not have proclaimed that Subhuti is a practitioner who delectates in *Aranyaic*[7] *cultivation*;[8] for in reality Subhuti does not cultivate anything; therefore Subhuti is dubbed as one who enjoys the practice of *Aranyaic cultivation.*"

Segment 10

[10-1]

The Buddha told Subhuti, "What do you make of this: did the *Thus-Adventist* make any *Obtainment* in the Dharma when he was at the place of Lamp-Lighting Buddha?"

Subhuti replied, "No, Your *World-Veneratedship*,

---

7. *Aranyaic*: from Sanskrit "*Aranya*," meaning forest; hence, hermitage.
8. *cultivation*: same as *practice*.

in reality, the *Thus-Adventist* did not make any *Obtainment* in the Dharma at the place of Lamp-Lighting Buddha."

[10-2]

"Subhuti," quoth the Buddha, "what do you make of this: do *Pusas majestify*[1] Buddha's Worlds?"

Subhuti replied, "No, Your *World-Veneratedship*. Why is it so? For the so-called '*majestifying the Buddha's Worlds*' is *Non-majestification*; therefore, it is named as *Majestification*."

"As a consequence," quoth the Buddha, "Subhuti, all *Pusa Mahasattvas* should generate the *Purified Heart* in such wise: they should not be attached to *Matter* while generating the *Heart*; nor should they be attached to *Sound*, *Smell*, *Taste*, *Tactile*, or *Dharma* while generating the

---

1. ***majestify***: to embellish and make magnificently beautiful. To get to this outcome would of course entail all the preparational procedures, such as cleaning and removing all the impurities (bad Karmas) at the outset. And so metaphorically it comes to mean to make betterments or improvements for Multibeings by leading them to practice the Dharma, so as to increase their true Well-beings (the "embellishments" with Buddhaic Merits).

Heart: they should not *reside* in any way while generating the *Heart*."

[10-3]

"Subhuti, metaphorically speaking, if there is someone with a stature in the size of the Sumeru Mount, would you consider his Stature as enormous?"

Subhuti replied, "Very much so, Your *World-Veneratedship*. Why is it so? For the Buddha says that it is *Non-stature*; therefore, it is termed as an *enormous Stature*."

Segment 11

"Subhuti," quoth the Buddha, "for instance, if there are the Ganges Rivers as many as the sands in the Ganges, would you deem the sands in all these Ganges as numerous?"

Subhuti replied, "Very much so, Your *World-*

Veneratedship; for merely the numbers of the rivers themselves are so numerous as to be uncountable, let alone the sands therein."

"Subhuti," quoth the Buddha, "right now I would like to impart this truth to you: if there be some virtuous men or virtuous women who would bestow on others seven kinds of jewelries as copious as would be sufficient to abound all over the aforesaid Gangesful-sand number of *Three Thousand Mega-thousand Worlds*, would these men or women acquire bountiful *Blissful Virtues*?"

Subhuti replied, "It would be quite bountiful indeed, Your *World-Veneratedship*."

The Buddha told Subhuti, "On the other hand, if certain virtuous men or virtuous women assimilate and uphold the Words in this *Sutra*, even as meager as a mere quatrain of *Gatha*, which they then relate to other people, the *Blissful Virtues* that the latter acquire is far superior to that which is acquired by the former."

Segment 12

"Furthermore," quoth the Buddha, "Subhuti, if someone converses about this *Sutra*, even as meager as a mere quatrain of *Gatha*, you should understand that this location of conversation ought to be made offerings to reverently by all *Worldly Beings*, *Celestial Beings*, and *Asuras*,[1] just as it is a Buddha's Temple or Stupa. It goes without saying that if someone can assimilate, uphold, recite, and incant this *Sutra*, Subhuti, you should know that this person will be fulfilling the first and foremost supreme rarest Dharma. Wherever this *Sutra* is situated, there will be the Buddha, as well as the Venerated Disciples of the Buddha."

---

1. *Asuras*: a genre of Celestial Beings, who enjoy very good Well-beings; but they are highly belligerent due to jealousy and anger, and so they are constantly at war with other Celestial Beings on that account.

Segment 13

[13-1]

At that time Subhuti said to the Buddha, "Your *World-Veneratedship*, how would this *Sutra* be entitled so that we can look up to and uphold it?"

The Buddha told Subhuti, "This *Sutra* will be called *Diamond Prajna-Paramita*. You should uphold it by this title. Why is it so? Subhuti, the *Prajna-paramita* that the Buddha enunciates is *Non-prajna-paramita*; thus it is denominated as *Prajna-paramita*."

[13-2]

"Subhuti, what do you make of this: has the *Thus-Adventist* enunciated any Dharma?"

Subhuti replied, "Your *World-Veneratedship*, the *Thus-Adventist* has not enunciated any."

The Buddha said, "Subhuti, what do you make of this: would the *Molecules* which constitute the *Three Thousand Mega-thousand Worlds* be considered as numerous?"

Subhuti said, "Very much so, Your *World-Veneratedship*."

"Yet Subhuti," quoth the Buddha, "the *Molecules* that the Buddha enunciates are *Non-molecules*; consequently, they are denominated as *Molecules*. Likewise, the *World* that the Buddha enunciates is *Non-world*; consequently, it is denominated as *World*."

[13-3]

"Subhuti, what do you make of this: could any-one perceive the *Thus-Adventist* by viewing His *Thirty-two Auspicious Physical Features*?"[1]

Subhuti replied, "No, Your *World-Veneratedship*, one could not perceive the *Thus-Adventist* by

---

1. ***Thirty-two Auspicious Physical Features***: The Buddha, through ages and ages of practice, has acquired some very extraordinary physical Features, which are deemed as very auspicious, such as the sign on the breast, the ear-lobes, which extend as long as to the shoulders, etc. These Features are auspicious in that if one contemplates in meditation on any of them, one could accumulate very good merits in the Karma through such meditation.

viewing His *Thirty-two Auspicious Physical Features*. Why is it so? For the *Thirty-two Features* that the *Thus-Adventist* enunciates are *Non-appearances*; consequently, they are de-nominated as *Thirty-two Features*."

"Subhuti," quoth the Buddha, "supposing that some virtuous men or virtuous women bestow their own *physical bodies* together with their *lives* to others for as numerous times as the sands in the Ganges; on the other hand, if some-one assimilates and upholds this *Sutra*, even as meager as a mere quatrain of *Gatha*, which he then relates to other people, the *Blissful Virtues* that the latter acquires is far more plenteous."

Segment 14

[14-1]

At that juncture, Subhuti, after hearing this *Sutra*, has deeply apprehended its significance and purport; and weeping bitter tears of sadness, he said to the Buddha, "It is extraordinary, Your *World-Veneratedship*. The *Sutra* that the Buddha has just divulged is of such profundity that even though I had long acquired the *Sagacious Eye*[1] in the past, I have never been able to be exposed to such a *Sutra*. Your *World-Veneratedship*, if someone, after hearing this *Sutra*, can engender *Purified Belief*, he will be able to realize the *Appearance of Reality*; if that be so, we would know that this man would be fulfilling the first and foremost extraordinary *Meritorious Virtues*. Your *World-Veneratedship*, the aforesaid *Reality* is of *Non-reality*; hence, the *Thus-Adventist* divulges that it is denominated as *Reality*."

[14-2]

"Your *World-Veneratedship*, at present I am still able to hear such a *Sutra*, and can believe, comprehend, assimilate and uphold without much difficulty. However, in the future, during *the Last*

1. *Sagacious Eye*: i.e., the Eye of Wisdom.

Cycle of five hundred years, suppose there is some *Multibeing*, who is still able to hear this *Sutra* with true *Belief*, *Comprehension*, *Assimilation* and *Sustenance*, this individual would surely be the most singularly unique person. Why is it so? For this person would not be fostering *Ego-appearance*, *Alter-appearance*, *Multibeing-appearance*, *and Lifespan-appearance*. How could it be so? For the *Ego-appearance* is actually *Non-appearance*. Likewise, the *Alter-appearance*, *Multibeing-appearance*, *and Lifespan-appearance* are all *Non-appearances*. Wherefore is it so? For those who are freed from all *Appearances* are to be entitled as Buddhas."

[14-3]

The Buddha told Subhuti, "Quite so, quite so. Meanwhile, if someone has heard this *Sutra* without being appalled, terrified or dismayed, you should be aware that such a person is utmostly rare. Why is it so? Subhuti, the *Supreme Paramita* that the *Thus-Adventist* has divulged is *Non-supreme-paramita*; therefore, it is de-nominated as the *Supreme Paramita*. Subhuti, the *Forbearance Paramita* that the Buddha has divulged is *Non-forbearance-paramita*; thus it is denominated as *Forbearance-paramita*. Why is it so? Subhuti, for instance, as in my past life, while I was being incised and mangled in the body by King Kali, at that moment, I was cherishing no *Ego-appearance*, *Alter-appearance*, *Multibeing-appearance*, and *Lifespan-appearance*. How would we know? For at that time while I was being mutilated joint by joint, had I still been cherishing *Ego-appearance*, *Alter-appearance*, *Multibeing-appearance*, and *Lifespan-appearance*, I should have turned hateful."

[14-4]

"Subhuti, again as I reminisce, in the past I had been a *Forbearant Sage*[2] for five hundred lifetimes, and during all that period I had been

---

2. **Forbearant Sage**: a practitioner practicing on *Forbearance*, which is very close to the Greek stoicism in ignoring the physical and spiritual pains or sufferings.

free from *Ego-appearance*, *Alter-appearance*, *Multibeing-appearance*, and *Lifespan-appearance*. Therefore, Subhuti, a *Pusa* must be freed from all *Appearances* while generating the *Anuttara-samyak-sambodhi Heart*: he must not *reside* in *Matter*[3] while generating the *Heart*; nor could he *reside* in *Sound, Smell, Taste, Tactile* or *Dharma* while generating the *Heart*. He should generate the *Un-residing Heart*. Should the *Heart* reside in any wise, it would be *Mal-residing*. Consequently, the Buddha says that the mind of a *Pusa* should not *reside* in *Matter* in his act of bestowing."

[14-5]

"Subhuti, for the sake of benefiting all Multibeings, a *Pusa* should do the *Bestowal* in such wise. The *Thus-Adventist* imparts that all and sundry *Appearances* are *Non-appearances*. Furthermore, he imparts that all and sundry

---

3. *Matter*: i.e., physical or tangible stuff.

Multibeings are *Non-multibeings*. Subhuti, the *Thus-Adventist* is a *Truth Sayer*, a *Veracity Sayer*, a *Thusness Sayer*, an *Undeceptive Sayer*, and an *Uncontradictory Sayer*. Subhuti, the Dharma that the *Thus-Adventist* has fulfilled is neither *Substantial* nor *Void*."

[14-6]

"Subhuti, if a *Pusa's* mind should reside in any *dharma*[4] while doing *Bestowals*, he would be likened to someone who enters into some pitch-dark chamber, as a result he would be unable to see anything. Contrarily, if a *Pusa's* mind would not *reside* in any dharma while doing *Bestowals*, he would be like someone endowed with *Eyes*, and in the meantime by the sunlight streaming brightly in, he would be able to perceive all the multifarious objects in the room.

"Subhuti, in the age that is to come, if some

---

4. *dharma*: This word with the first letter in lower case (dharma) stands for "all beings," or anything in existence; whereas "Dharma" with a capitalized first letter usually stands for Buddha Dharma, or Buddha's Doctrines.

virtuous men or virtuous women are able to accept, uphold, read, and incant this *Sutra*, the *Thus-Adventist* will by his Buddhaic *Noesis*[5] know all about these persons, and perceive all about these persons in that they will all be fulfilling infinite boundless *Meritorious Virtues*."

Segment 15

[15-1]

"Subhuti," quoth the Buddha, "suppose some virtuous men or virtuous women would bestow their own physical bodies as numerous as the sands in the Ganges to others during the *ante meridiem*; while in the noontime they would also bestow their own physical bodies as numerous as the sands in the Ganges; and during the *post*

---

5. *Noesis*: the highest Wisdom of Buddhas or high-status *Pusas*. This term originally came from Greek, was first used in <u>Platonism</u> to mean the highest kind of knowledge or knowledge of eternal forms or ideas, and later used in <u>Husserl</u> to denote something else. From now on, this term will be employed to denote the Consummate Wisdom of Buddha or other Enlightened saints.

meridiem they would still bestow their own physical bodies as numerous as the sands in the Ganges. In this wise, throughout myriads of millions and billions of *Kalpas'* time, they would have made innumerable *bestowals* with their physical bodies. Whereas, on the other hand, suppose someone on hearing this *Sutra*, would nurture Belief in it without any defiance, his *Well-beings* are much superior to the previous ones on this account; let alone copying and writing, assimilating and upholding, reciting and incanting, as well as relating and expounding it to others."

[15-2]

"In fine, Subhuti, this *Sutra* is embodied with inconceivable, ineffable, unweighable, immeasurable, boundless *Meritorious Virtues*. It is a *Sutra* that the *Thus-Adventist* imparts not only for those who have generated the *Major-vehicle*[1]

---

1. **Major-vehicle**: i.e., the *Vehicle* of Mahayana, which can accommodate a great number of people (that is, benefiting numerous people), as

Heart, but especially for those who have generated the *Supreme-vehicle Heart*. If someone who can assimilate, uphold, recite and incant, and also extensively relate this to others, the *Thus-Adventist* will assuredly know all about this person, and perceive all about this person in the fact that he is bound to fulfill immeasurable, unweighable, confineless, inconceivable *Meritorious Virtues*. Such a person as this is one that will be *shouldering* the *Loads* of the *Thus-Adventist's Anuttara-samyak-sambodhi*. Wherefore would it be so? Subhuti, if a person takes delight in *Minor Dharmas*,[2] he would be attached to *Ego Views*, *Alter Views*, *Multibeing Views*, *and Lifespan Views*, to the effect that he would not be able to hear, assimilate, recite, incant, or expound this *Sutra* to others."

---

opposed to Hinayana, which generally aims at *Self-deliverance* as the final goal, benefiting none other than the practitioner himself—once with his goal achieved, he would never come back again, leaving all the unenlightened beings to be on their own.

2. **Minor Dharmas**: i.e., the doctrines of Hinayana and other Worldly teachings, or Externalist doctrines (that is, the teachings of other religions).

[15-3]

"Subhuti, wheresoever this *Sutra* is located, all the Terrestrial Beings, Celestial Deities, and *Asuras*³ ought to make offerings over there, and you should be aware that that same locale *is* a *Stupa*, to which all *Multibeings* should reverently pay homage, make *Perambulations*⁴ around it, and disperse flowers and incense to it as well."

Segment 16

[16-1]

"Furthermore, Subhuti," quoth the Buddha, "when some virtuous men or virtuous women are assimilating, upholding, reciting and incanting this *Sutra*, and while doing so, if they should still be disparaged or spurned by others, these good people's sinful Karmas derived from their

---

3. *Asuras*: See Note 1 in Segment 12.
4. *Perambulations*: i.e., walking meditation around a stupa, shrine or person, as one of the highest form of showing respect to Buddha, holy people, or elders.

past lives, which should be causing them to de-generate into the *Vile Realms*[1] in the immediate next life, will all be obliterated, simply due to the *Retributions* of their being disparaged and spurned by people in this life. Furthermore, these people are of a surety to attain the *Anuttara-samyak-sambodhi*."

[16-2]

"Subhuti, as I reminisce that in the past myriads of *Asamkhyas*[2] of *Kalpas*,[3] prior to Lamp-Lighting Buddha, I was able to meet with eight hundred four thousand billion *nayuta*[4] Buddhas, and that to all of them I was able to make offerings, and attend upon them, without frittering any time away in vain. Nevertheless, suppose someone in the future *fin de siècle*[5] can assimilate, uphold, recite, and incant this *Sutra*, the *Meritorious Virtues*

---

1. *Vile Realms*: i.e., the Three Vile Realms: Purgatory (Hell), Starving Ghost, and Animal.
2. *Asamkhyas*: innumerable, countless; said to be about trillions of trillions.
3. *Kalpa*: aeon, a very long long time.
4. *nayuta*: one million, or ten million.
5. *fin de siècle*: French, end of the century (or age), or the later-age.

that he will be acquiring, as compared with what I had gained in making offerings to the Buddhas, would be one hundred times more, or one thousand million billion times more, or even to the point of being undepictable by any numerals or similes.

"Subhuti, in the future *fin de siècle*, if some virtuous men or virtuous women could assimilate, uphold, recite, and incant this *Sutra*, the *Meritorious Virtues* to be acquired, which if I divulge in full, and if ever some people should happen to hear of it, they will of a surety go berserk, and become so vulpinely skeptical that they would never believe it for a minute. You should be aware that the imports of this *Sutra* are inconceivable and ineffable, and as a consequence the *Retributional Deserts* are also thus inconceivable and inexpressible."

Segment 17

[17-1]

At that juncture Subhuti said to the Buddha, "Your *World-Veneratedship*, when virtuous men or virtuous women have generated the *Anuttara-samyak-sambodhi Heart*, how should they *reside*? And how should they *subjugate* their own minds?"

The Buddha told Subhuti, "When virtuous men or virtuous women have generated the *Anuttara-samyak-sambodhi Heart*, they should engender such Mind: 'I should salvage all the Multibeings into *Nirvana*, and after having salvaged all the Multibeings, I should be aware that there was actually not even one single individual that I have ever salvaged.' Why is it so? For if a *Pusa* fosters *Ego-appearance*, *Alter-appearance*, *Multibeing-appearance*, *and Lifespan-appearance*, he would not be a *Pusa*. What is the reason for this? Subhuti, for *in Reality* there is no such Dharma as called *the Generation of Anuttara-samyak-sambodhi Heart.*"

[17-2]

"Subhuti, what do you make of this: at the place of Lamp-Lighting Buddha did the *Thus-Adventist* obtain any Dharma therewith to acquire *Anuttara-samyak-sambodhi*?"

Subhuti replied, "No, Your *World-Veneratedship.* If I comprehend correctly the import of what the Buddha has just imparted: at the place of Lamp-Lighting Buddha, the Buddha did not obtain any Dharma therewith to acquire *Anuttara-samyak-sambodhi.*"

The Buddha said, "Quite so, quite so. *In Reality* there is no Dharma called '*the Thus-Adventist attaining Anuttara-samyak-sambodhi.*' Subhuti, if ever there were a Dharma called '*the Thus-Adventist obtaining Anuttara-samyak-sambodhi,*' the Lamp-Lighting Buddha would not have conferred on me *the Prognosticative Ordination*[1] by

---

1. *Prognosticative Ordination*: a Buddha's solemn and formal prophesy

saying: 'In the future age, thou shalt become a Buddha, with the appellation of Shakyamuni.' Simply because in reality there was no Dharma called *'the obtainment of Anuttara-samyak-sambodhi'*, in consequence of that, the Lamp-Lighting Buddha conferred on me the *Prognosticative Ordination* by pronouncing thus: 'In the future age thou shalt become a Buddha, with the appellation of Shakyamuni.' Wherefore is it so? The term *'Thus-Adventist'* denotes the import that all *dharmas* in reality are in the state of *Thusness*."

[17-3]

"If someone should say that the *Thus-Adventist* has obtained *Anuttara-samyak-sambodhi*, Subhuti, it should be known that in Reality there is no Dharma called *'the Buddha obtaining Anuttara-samyak-sambodhi.'* Subhuti, in

---

and promise to someone about his candidacy for the attainment of Buddhahood in the future, usually with the details as to the date, the Appellation of the Buddha, his family, his important disciples, and the duration of his Dharmas.

the *Anuttara-samyak-sambodhi* that the *Thus-Adventist* has fulfilled, it is neither *substantial* nor *void*. In consequence, the *Thus-Adventist* imparts that all *dharmas* are *Buddhaic Dharmas*. Subhuti, the so-called 'all *dharmas*' are not *all dharmas*; therefore they come to be denominated as 'all dharmas.'"

[17-4]

"Subhuti, for instance, if there is someone who is tall and huge in stature…."

Subhuti remarked, "Your *World-Veneratedship*, the tall and huge stature that the *Thus-Adventist* refers to is no huge stature; therefore, it is named as 'huge stature.'"

"Subhuti," quoth the Buddha, "it is exactly the same with the *Pusa*: if he should make such a pronouncement as 'I will *nirvanize* myriads of *Multibeings*,' he would not have been entitled to a *Pusa*. Wherefore is it so? Subhuti, for there is no Dharma named *Pusa*. Accordingly, the Buddha imparts that all *dharmas* are devoid of *Ego*, devoid of *Alter*, devoid of *Multibeing*, and devoid of *Lifespan*."

[17-5]

"Subhuti, if a *Pusa* should make such proclamations as 'I will *majestify* the Buddha World,' he would not have been entitled to a *Pusa*. Why is it so? The *majestification* of the Buddha World that the *Thus-Adventist* enunciates is no *Majestification*; therefore, it is denominated as *Majestification*. Subhuti, if a *Pusa* has thoroughly apprehended *the Dharma of Egolessness*, the *Thus-Adventist* will then pronounce that he is entitled to a genuine *Pusa*."

Segment 18

[18-1]

"Subhuti," quoth the Buddha, "what do you make of this: does the *Thus-Adventist* have *Naked*

Eyes?"

"Just so," replied Subhuti, "Your *World-Veneratedship*, the *Thus-Adventist* does have *Naked Eye*s."

"Subhuti," quoth the Buddha, "what do you make of this: does the *Thus-Adventist* have *Celestial Eyes*?"

"Just so," replied Subhuti, "Your *World-Veneratedship*, the *Thus-Adventist* does have *Celestial Eyes*."

"Subhuti," quoth the Buddha, "what do you make of this: does the *Thus-Adventist* have *Sagacious Eyes*?"

"Just so," replied Subhuti, "Your *World-Veneratedship*, the *Thus-Adventist* does have *Sagacious Eyes*."

"Subhuti," quoth the Buddha, "what do you make of this: does the *Thus-Adventist* have *Dharmic Eyes*?"

"Just so," replied Subhuti, "Your *World-Veneratedship*, the *Thus-Adventist* does have *Dharmic Eyes*."

"Subhuti," quoth the Buddha, "what do you make of this: does the *Thus-Adventist* have *Buddhaic Eyes*?"

"Just so," replied Subhuti, "Your *World-Veneratedship*, the *Thus-Adventist* does have *Buddhaic Eyes*."[1]

[18-2]

"Subhuti," quoth the Buddha, "what do you make of this: does the Buddha say that all the sands in the Ganges are sands?"

"Just so," replied Subhuti, "Your *World-Veneratedship*, the *Thus-Adventist* does say that they are sands."

---

1. *Naked Eyes*, *Celestial Eyes*, *Sagacious Eyes*, *Dharmic Eyes*, *Buddhaic Eyes*: These are the well-known *Five Eyes* of the Buddha, which connote the idea that the Buddha would never "abandon" any Multibeings of any status until they have eventually reached the Ultimate Enlightenment.

"Subhuti," quoth the Buddha, "what do you make of this: suppose that there are the Ganges Rivers whose numbers are as many as the sands in the Ganges, and in turn, when the Buddha-Worlds are as many as the sands in those Ganges Rivers, would these Worlds be deemed as numerous?"

"Very much so, Your *World-Veneratedship*," replied Subhuti.

The Buddha told Subhuti, "The all and sundry Minds of all the *Multibeings* in those Gangesful-sand number of Buddha-Worlds—the *Thus-Adventist* perceives them all perspicuously. Why is it so? For the *Minds* that the *Thus-Adventist* enunciates are *no Minds*; therefore, they are denominated as *Minds*. What is the reason for this? Subhuti, for *the Past Minds* are unobtainable; the *Present Minds* are unobtainable; the *Future Minds* are unobtainable."

Segment 19

"Subhuti," quoth the Buddha, "what do you make of this: suppose someone is to make Bestowals with seven kinds of jewelries, which are so copious as to be able to abound the *Three Thousand Mega-thousand Worlds*, would the *Blisses* that this person is to acquire through this act be plenteous?"

"Just so," replied Subhuti, "Your *World-Veneratedship*, the *Bliss* that this person is to acquire from this cause will be quite plenteous."

"Subhuti," quoth the Buddha, "if *Blissful Virtues* be *substantial* in *Reality*, the *Thus-Adventist* would not say that the *Blissful Virtues* acquired are plenteous. Due to the fact that the *Blissful Virtues* are *unsubstantial*, hence the *Thus-Adventist* imparts that the *Blissful Virtues* acquired are plenteous."

Segment 20

"Subhuti," quoth the Buddha, "what do you make of this: could the Buddha be perceived by means of His *Consummate Physical Body*?"

Subhuti replied, "No, Your *World-Veneratedship*. The *Thus-Adventist* should not be perceived by means of His physical body. Why is it so? The *Consummate Physical Body* that the *Thus-Adventist* enunciates is no *Consummate Physical Body*; therefore, it is named as the *Consummate Physical Body*."

"Subhuti," quoth the Buddha, "what do you make of this: could the *Thus-Adventist* be perceived by means of His *Consummate Appearances*?"

Subhuti replied, "No, Your *World-Veneratedship*. The *Thus-Adventist* should not be perceived by means of *Consummate Appearances*. Why is it so? The *Consummate Appearance* that the *Thus-Adventist* enunciates are *not consummate*; hence they are denominated as *Consummate*

Appearances."

Segment 21

"Subhuti," quoth the Buddha, "never will you say that the *Thus-Adventist* makes such an *Ideation* as 'I will impart some Dharmas.' Do not ever make such an *Ideation*. Why is it so? If someone says that the *Thus-Adventist* has imparted some Dharmas, he is calumniating the Buddha, for this person cannot apprehend what I have divulged. Subhuti, the so-called '*Dharma-imparting*' would only signify that there are no *Dharmas* to be imparted, and as such it could be denominated as *the Impartation of the Dharma*."

At that juncture Subhuti *the Sagacious Life*,[1] asked the Buddha, "Your *World-Veneratedship*, are there going to be Multibeings in future ages

---

1. *the Sagacious Life*: This is the meritorious Epithet that Subhuti had earned due to his outstanding wisdom.

who after hearing this Dharma could generate *Faith*?"

The Buddha said, "Subhuti, they are not *Multibeings*, nor *Non-multibeings*. Why is it so? Subhuti, for the so-called *Multibeings-Multibeings* that the *Thus-Adventist* enunciates are Non-multibeings; thus they are denominated as Multibeings."

Segment 22

Subhuti said to the Buddha, "Your *World-Veneratedship*, in the *Anuttara-samyak-sam-bodhi* that the Buddha has fulfilled, is there nothing obtained?"

"Quite so, quite so," quoth the Buddha, "Subhuti, in the *Anuttara-samyak-sambodhi* that I have fulfilled, there is not even an iota of Dharma to be obtainable; such state is denominated as *Anuttara-samyak-sambodhi*."

Segment 23

"Furthermore, Subhuti," quoth the Buddha, "this Dharma is entirely *equitable*, without any differentiation in terms of the status of either high or low; such state is denominated as *Anuttara-samyak-sambodhi*. Moreover, when someone applies *Egolessness, Alterlessness, Multibeing-lessness, and Lifespanlessness* as a means to the cultivation of all other Good Dharmas, he is sure to fulfil *Anuttara-samyak-sambodhi*. Subhuti, the so-called *Good Dharmas* that the *Thus-Adventist* enunciates are *Non-good-dharmas*; hence they are denominated as *Good Dharmas*."

Segment 24

"Subhuti," quoth the Buddha, "suppose someone makes *Bestowals* to others with a vast hoard of seven kinds of jewelries, which could be piled up as high as all the Sumeru Mounts in the

Three Thousand Mega-thousand Worlds. On the other hand, supposing someone else assimilates, upholds and relates just a little portion of this *Prajna-Paramita Sutra* to others, even though as meager as a mere quatrain of *Gatha*, the *Felicific Virtues* that the former person gains, as compared with that which acquired by the latter one, would not be even close to one hundredth of it, nor one thousand-million-billionth of it, nor even to the point of being depictable by any numerals or metaphors."

Segment 25

"Subhuti," quoth the Buddha, "what do you make of this: you good people here should never say that the *Thus-Adventist* makes such an *Ideation* as 'I should salvage the *Multibeings*'?

"Subhuti, do not ever conceive such a Notion. Wherefore would it be so? For in Reality there are no Multibeings that are salvaged by the *Thus-Adventist*. Should there be any Multibeings salvaged by the *Thus-Adventist*, the *Thus-Adventist* must have fostered *Ego*, *Alter*, *Multibeings, and Lifespan*. Subhuti, the *Ego* that the *Thus-Adventist* enunciates is *Non-ego*; and yet the *Common Plebeians*[1] do take *Egos* to be actually in existence. Subhuti, the so-called '*Common Plebeians*' that the *Thus-Adventist* enunciates are *Non-common-plebeians*; thus they are denominated as *Common Plebeians*."

Segment 26

"Subhuti," quoth the Buddha, "what do you make of this: could one contemplate on the *Thus-Adventist* by means of His *Thirty-two Auspicious Features*?"

Subhuti said, "Just so, just so; one could con-

---

1. **Common Plebeians**: ordinary unenlightened people.

template on the *Thus-Adventist* by means of His *Thirty-two Auspicious Features*."

The Buddha said, "Subhuti, if the *Thus-Adventist* could be contemplated on by means of the *Thirty-two Auspicious Features*, a *Wheel-revolving Anointed King*[1] might as well be deemed as a *Thus-Adventist*."

Subhuti then said to the Buddha, "Your *World-Veneratedship*, if I comprehend correctly the import that the Buddha has just imparted, I would say that one must not contemplate on the *Thus-Adventist* by means of the *Thirty-two Auspicious Features*."

At this juncture the *World-Venerated One* divulged this *Gatha*:

> "If a person views Me through *Matter*,
> Or seeks after Me by means of Voices,

---

1. ***Wheel-revolving Anointed King***: In Hindu folklore, a mighty emperor who ruled a vast kingdom with beneficence, rather than by force, and who was loved and respected universally—such a great sovereign or benign ruler was called a Wheel-revolving Anointed King.

**What this person practices is merely the Devious
Way,**

And so he shall not be able to perceive the *Ju-lai*."[2]

Segment 27

"Subhuti," quoth the Buddha, "if you should conceive such a *Notion* as 'The *Thus-Adventist* has realized *Anuttara-samyak-sambodhi* without needing the attributes of the *Consummate Features*.' Subhuti, never conceive such a *Notion* as 'The *Thus-Adventist* does not need the *Consummate Features* to realize *Anuttara-samyak-sambodhi*.' Subhuti, should you conceive such a Notion while generating the *Anuttara-samyak-sambodhi Heart*, you would be as good as pronouncing that all *dharmas* are to undergo *Nihilistic Extinction*. Never will you conceive such a *Notion*. Wherefore is it so? For

---

2. ***Ju-lai***: the Chinese translation (or rendition) of the Sanskrit *Tathagata*, meaning: the Thus-Adventist (Thus-Comer).

anyone that has generated the *Anuttara-samyak-sambodhi Heart* should never construe that the *dharmas* are to be of *Nihilistically Extinctive Appearances*."

Segment 28

"Subhuti," quoth the Buddha, "supposing that a *Pusa* is to bestow on others seven kinds of jewelries, which are as bountiful as to abound the Gangesful-sand Worlds. On the other hand, if someone else could comprehend that all *dharmas* are devoid of *Ego*, whereby he succeeds in the attainment of *Forbearance*. Thus the *Meritorious Virtues* that the latter *Pusa* has acquired are far superior to that which gained by the former one. Wherefore would it be so? Subhuti, this is simply due to the fact that *Pusas* would not hold *Blissful Virtues*."

Subhuti asked the Buddha, "Your *World-*

Veneratedship, why is it that *Pusas* would not hold *Blissful Virtues*?"

"Subhuti," quoth the Buddha, "a *Pusa* is not supposed to become avid and attached to the *Blissful Virtues* that he has cultivated. Hence, it is said that he would not hold *Blissful Virtues*."

Segment 29

"Subhuti," quoth the Buddha, "if someone professes that the *Thus-Adventist* manifests Himself either in coming or going, either in sitting or reclining; it would only show that this person could not comprehend the *Purports* that I have tried to impart. Why is it so? For the so-called '*Thus-Adventist*' signifies '*neither coming from somewhere, nor leaving for anywhere*'; such a state is denominated as '*the Thus-Adventist*.'"

Segment 30

"Subhuti," quoth the Buddha, "suppose some virtuous men or virtuous women would granulate the *Three Thousand Mega-thousand Worlds* into *molecules*; what do you make of this: would those *molecules* be numerous?"

Subhuti replied, "Very much so, Your *World-Veneratedship*. Wherefore is it so? For if those *molecules* were of *Real Substantiality*, the Buddha would not have called them *Molecules*. Wherefore is it so? For the *Molecules* that the Buddha enunciates are *Non-molecules*; hence they are denominated as *Molecules*. Your *World-Veneratedship*, the *Three Thousand Mega-thousand Worlds* that the *Thus-Adventist* enunciates are *Non-worlds*; hence they are denominated as *Worlds*. Why is it so? For if the World be of *Real Substantiality*, it would be of *Uni-amalgamated Holism*.[1] The *Uni-amalgam-*

---

1. **Uni-amalgamated Holism**: In the Worldly people's eye, everything appears to be "an *indivisible* whole," although they are, as a matter of

ated Holism that the *Thus-Adventist* enunciates is *Non-uniamalgamated Holism*; hence it is denominated as *Uni-amalgamated Holism*."

"Subhuti," quoth the Buddha, "actually the so-called *Uni-amalgamated Holism* is unutterable; yet the *Common Plebeians* are avaricious and strongly attached to that matter."

---

fact, put together (or assembled) by various *discrete parts*. This is especially true of beings with life, either animated (animals) or inanimated (plants). Ordinary people tend to view things of life as an "Organism," which they would presume to be *an indivisible whole*, and therefore would consider them as not subject to changes. And so these people are, as it were, *justified* in being attached to their own Ego, so as to stay as what they are, to be complacent with themselves, to enjoy and pamper their own *status quo*, and finally to refuse to improve or cultivate themselves in whatever way. As a result, they would become so attached to *their own image* (*Ego-appearance*) that they would generally detest, reject, or repel anything disparate from their Ego, such as other individuals (*Alter*), or other people collectively (*Multibeings*). And this is the fundamental cause for all the *delusive differentiations* in life, whereby all the worries, and eventually afflictions and pains in life come into being. These problems all derive from the conviction of the specious *Holism*, which is, to a major degree, responsible for most kinds of conceptual ignorance.

Segment 31

"Subhuti," quoth the Buddha, "if someone professes that the Buddha has expounded the *Ego Views, the Alter View, the Multibeing View, and the Lifespan View.* Subhuti, what do make of this: does this person apprehend the purport that I have tried to impart?"

"No," replied Subhuti, "Your *World-Veneratedship*, this person could not apprehend the purport that the *Thus-Adventist* has tried to impart. Why is it so? For the *Ego View, Alter View, Multibeing View and Lifespan View* that the *World-Venerated One* divulges are *Non-ego-view, Non-alter-view, Non-multibeing-view*, and *Non-lifespan-view*; thus they are denominated as *Ego View, Alter View, Multibeing View and Lifespan View.*"

"Subhuti," quoth the Buddha, "anyone who has generated the *Anuttara-samyak-sambodhi Heart* should comprehend all the dharmas in this way, should perceive them in this way, should believe and explicate them in this way, to the effect that he would not *engender* any *Dharmic Appearances* in those *Cultivations*. Subhuti, with respect to the so-called '*Dharmic Appearances*,' the *Thus-Adventist* has pronounced them to be *Non-dharmic-appearances*; hence they are denominated as *Dharmic Appearances*."

Segment 32

[32-1]

"Subhuti," quoth the Buddha, "suppose someone is to make Bestowals to others with seven kinds of jewelries, which are so copious as to be able to abound uncountable *Asamkhya* Worlds. Whereas, if some virtuous men or virtuous women who have generated the *Bodhi-Heart* could take the Words of this *Sutra*, even as meager as a mere quatrain of *Gatha*, which they would assimilate, uphold, recite, incant, and then expound for others, the *Well-beings* that they could acquire would be far superior to that which the former could gain. Furthermore, how should one expound the Dharma to others? In expounding the Dharma, one should not *seize upon* any *Appearances*, so that one could maintain the *Immotivity*[1] of *Thus-thusness*.[2] Wherefore could it be so?

"All the *Dharmas of Implementations*[3]

Are just like a Dream, a *Phantasm*, a Bubble, or a Shadow,

They also bear likeness to Dew-drops or Electricity;

One should contemplate upon all things in this wise."

---

1. *Immotivity*: unmovableness; impregnability.
2. *Thus-thusness*: The repetition of the word "thus" connotes the state of "thusness" in two ways: the *Interior Thusness* and the *Exterior Thusness*. Specifically, it means the perfect Enlightenment that both the *interior* (mind-body-speech) and the *exterior* (the surrounding external objects and living Beings) are in the quality of "*thusness*"; hence this is called the state of "Thus-thusness." (Cf. Chinese Ju-Ju, 如如.)
3. *Dharmas of Implementations*: i.e., all the mundane things or beings, for the fact that they are the outcome and effect of all sorts of "workings" (implementations).

[32-2]

When the Buddha has finished divulging this *Sutra*, Elder Subhuti and the other *Bhiksus*, *Bhiksunis*,[4] *Upasakas*,[5] and *Upasikas*,[6] as well as all the *Terrestrial* and *Celestial Beings* and *Asuras*, having heard what the Buddha has just divulged, all exalted jubilantly; and they all believed, assimilated, and would practice it deferentially.

End of *The Diamond Prajna-Paramita Sutra.*

Translated on: 1/18/2001 at AB Temple, Michigan, USA

Final Revision: 5/5/2005 at MV Temple, Taipei, Taiwan

Revision for 2nd Edition: 2/1/2007 at MV Temple, Taipei, Taiwan

---

4. ***Bhiksunis***: ordained Buddhist nuns.
5. ***Upasakas***: Buddhist male lay practitioners who have officially taken the Five-Precept Vows in a ceremony presided by a qualified Bhiksu in a shrine hall.
6. ***Upasikas***: Buddhist female lay practitioners who have officially taken the Five-Precept Vows in a ceremony presided by a qualified Bhiksu in a shrine hall.

The Dedicatory Gatha

I wish to abolish the Three Impediments,
And to obtain Wisdom, thereby to achieve
mental perspicuity.
I also wish people universally to diminish and
exterminate all their Sinful Impediments,
And all of us to practice the Pusa's Way in all
our future Lives to come.

金剛般若波羅蜜經

姚秦三藏法師鳩摩羅什譯

毘盧出版社 敬印

「法海譯叢」英譯三經
出版引言

　　爲令正法昌隆，廣大利益全世界無量有緣眾生，本寺住持上成下觀法師業已將數部佛經英譯完成，並取名爲「法海譯叢」。就中「四十二章經」、「金剛經」、「六祖壇經」三部業已排版即將完成，準備付梓，各印數千冊。唯願十方善信共同發心，推動此無上殊勝如來法身事業。此三經出版後，擬免費贈送全球各國首都、主要大都市、大學圖書館及佛教道場，以爲無量有情共種無上菩提善根。是故助印功德無量。

　　又，此三經者係各爲「第一」經典：

(1) 佛說四十二章經──係於東漢明帝時白馬馱來，爲中土第一部漢譯之佛經。斯爲此經之「第一」，意義重大。而今上成下觀法師將此經英譯，亦第一部印出，其意義亦非同小可。

(2) 金剛經──爲大般若經六百部中最重要的一分，斯爲其「第一」；且此經於禪宗自六祖大師以來，即爲祖師及禪者印心之依據，故亦爲其「第一」

者也。

(3) 六祖法寶壇經——中國佛教最大的成就，眾所公
　　認即禪宗之發揚；而禪宗之所以得發揚光大者，
　　厥在六祖惠能大師之殊勝功德與因緣。是故中華
　　禪宗自六祖大師起，即以兩部要典爲宗：(一)金
　　剛經、(二)六祖壇經，宋朝以後又再加上「傳
　　燈錄」。是故「六祖壇經」在禪門修習中，除
　　金剛經外，蓋居於首要之地位。斯爲此經之「第
　　一」。

由於以上三經，各以其要，而居「第一」，是故助印
如是經典，所獲福德不可思量。

　　復次，依優婆塞戒經，印經法施之功德殊勝無
比，茲引經文如下，以爲諸善信參考、依教修行：
「善男子，施有二種：一者法施，二者財施。法
施則得財法二報，財施唯還得財寶報……財施名
下，法施名上。云何法施？若有比丘、比丘尼、
優婆塞、優婆夷，能教他人具信、戒、施、多
聞、智慧，若以紙墨令人書寫，若自書寫如來正
典，然後施人令得讀誦，是名法施。如是施者，
未來無量世中得好上色。何以故？眾生聞法斷除
瞋心，以是因緣，施主未來無量世中得成上色。

眾生聞法慈心不殺，以是因緣，施主未來無量世中得壽命長。眾生聞法不盜他財，以是因緣，施主未來無量世中多饒財寶。眾生聞已開心樂施，以是因緣，施主未來無量世中身得大力。眾生聞法斷諸放逸，以是因緣，施主未來無量世中身得安樂。眾生聞法斷除癡心，以是因緣，施主未來無量世中得無礙辯。眾生聞法生信無疑，以是因緣，施主未來無量世中信心明了。戒、施、聞、慧，亦復如是；是故法施勝於財施。」（優婆塞戒經雜品第十九）

釋成觀 識於台北大毘盧寺
2005.2.18

南無本師釋迦牟尼佛 <small>三稱</small>

開經偈

無上甚深微妙法

百千萬劫難遭遇

我今見聞得受持

願解如來眞實義

金剛般若波羅蜜經

姚秦三藏法師鳩摩羅什譯

法會因由分第一

如是我聞：一時佛在舍衛國祇樹給孤獨園，與大比丘眾千二百五十人俱。爾時世尊食時，著衣持鉢，入舍衛大城乞食。於其城中次第乞已，還至本處。飯食訖，收衣鉢、洗足已，敷座而坐。

善現啓請分第二

時長老須菩提，在大眾中，即從座起，偏袒右肩、右膝著地，合掌恭敬而白佛言：「希有世尊，如來善護念諸菩薩，善付囑諸菩薩。世尊，善男子、善女人發阿耨多羅三藐三菩提心，云何應住？

云何降伏其心？」佛言：「善哉善哉！須菩提，如汝所說：如來善護念諸菩薩，善付囑諸菩薩。汝今諦聽，當為汝說。善男子、善女人發阿耨多羅三藐三菩提心，應如是住，如是降伏其心。」「唯然世尊，願樂欲聞。」

大乘正宗分第三

佛告須菩提：「諸菩薩摩訶薩應如是降伏其心：所有一切眾生之類——若卵生、若胎生、若濕生、若化生，若有色、若無色，若有想、若無想，若非有想、非無想——我皆令入無餘涅槃而滅度之。如是滅度無量無數無邊眾生，實無眾生得滅度者。何以故？須菩提，若菩薩有我相、人相、眾生相、壽者相，即非菩薩。」

妙行無住分第四

「復次，須菩提，菩薩於法應無所住，行於布施。所謂不住色布施，不住聲、香、味、觸、法布施。須菩提，菩薩應如是布施，不住於相。何以故？若菩薩不住相布施，其福德不可思量。須菩提，於意云何？東方虛空可思量不？」「不也，世尊。」「須菩提，南西北方、四維上下虛空，可思量不？」「不也，世尊。」「須菩提，菩薩無住相布施，福德亦復如是不可思量。須菩提，菩薩但應如所教住。」

如理實見分第五

「須菩提，於意云何？可以身相見如來

不？」「不也，世尊。不可以身相得見如來。何以故？如來所說身相，即非身相。」佛告須菩提：「凡所有相，皆是虛妄；若見諸相非相，即見如來。」

正信希有分第六

須菩提白佛言：「世尊，頗有眾生，得聞如是言說章句，生實信不？」佛告須菩提：「莫作是說！如來滅後，後五百歲，有持戒修福者，於此章句能生信心，以此為實。當知是人，不於一佛、二佛、三四五佛而種善根，已於無量千萬佛所，種諸善根。聞是章句，乃至一念生淨信者，須菩提，如來悉知悉見。是諸眾生，得如是無量福德。何以故？是諸眾生無復我相、人相、眾生相、壽者相，無法相、亦無非法相。何以故？是諸眾生若心取相，即為著我、人、眾生、壽者；若取法相，即著我、人、眾生、壽者。何以故？若取非法相，即著我、人、眾生、壽者。是故不應取法、不應取非法。以是義故，如來常說：汝等比丘，知我說法如筏喻者，法尚應捨，何況非法！」

無得無說分第七

「須菩提，於意云何？如來得阿耨多羅三藐三菩提耶？如來有所說法耶？」須菩提言：「如我解佛所說義，無有定法名阿耨多羅三藐三菩提，亦無有定法如來可說。何以故？如來所說法，皆不可取、不可說，非法、非非法。所以者何？一切賢聖皆以無爲法而有差別。」

依法出生分第八

「須菩提，於意云何？若人滿三千大千世界七寶，以用布施，是人所得福德，寧爲多不？」須菩提言：「甚多，世尊。何以故？是福德、即非福德性，是故如來說福德多。」「若復有人，於此經中受持乃至四句偈等，爲他人說，其福勝彼。何以故？須菩提，一切諸佛、及諸佛阿耨多羅三藐三菩提法，皆從此經出。須菩提，所謂佛、法者，即非佛、法，是名佛、法。」

一相無相分第九

「須菩提，於意云何？須陀洹能作是念：『我得須陀洹果』不？」須菩提言：「不也，世尊。何以故？須陀洹名爲入流，而無所入——不入色、聲、香、味、觸、法——是名須陀洹。」

「須菩提，於意云何？斯陀含能作是念：『我得斯陀含果』不？」須菩提言：「不也，世尊。何以故？斯陀含名一往來，而實無往來，是名斯陀含。」

「須菩提，於意云何？阿那含能作是念：『我得阿那含果』不？」須菩提言：「不也，世尊。何以故？阿那含名爲不來，而實無不來，是故名阿那含。」「須菩提，於意云何？阿羅漢能作是念：『我得阿羅漢道』不？」須菩提言：「不也，世尊。何以故？實無有法名阿羅漢。世尊，若阿羅漢作是念：

『我得阿羅漢道』，即爲著我、人、眾生、壽者。世尊，佛說我得無諍三昧，人中最爲第一，是第一離欲阿羅漢。世尊，我不作是念：『我是離欲阿羅漢』。世尊，我若作是念：『我得阿羅漢道』，世尊則不說：『須菩提是樂阿蘭那行者』。以須菩提實無所行，而名須菩提是樂阿蘭那行。」

莊嚴淨土分第十

佛告須菩提：「於意云何？如來昔在然燈佛所，於法有所得不？」「不也，世尊。如來在然燈佛所，於法實無所得。」「須菩提，於意云何？菩薩莊嚴佛土不？」「不也，世尊。何以故？莊嚴佛土者，即非莊嚴，是名莊嚴。」

「是故須菩提，諸菩薩摩訶薩應如是生清淨心——不應住色生心，不應住聲、香、味、觸、法生心，應無所住而生其心。須菩提，譬如有人，身如須彌山王；於意云何？是身為大不？」須菩提言：「甚大，世尊。何以故？佛說非身，是名大身。」

無爲福勝分第十一

「須菩提，如恒河中所有沙數，如是沙等恒河，於意云何？是諸恒河沙，寧爲多不？」須菩提言：「甚多，世尊。但諸恒河，尚多無數，何況其沙？」「須菩提，我今實言告汝：若有善男子、善女人，以七寶滿爾所恒河沙數三千大千世界，以用布施，得福多不？」須菩提言：「甚多，世尊。」佛告須菩提：
「若善男子、善女人，於此經中、乃至
受持四句偈等，爲他人說，而此福德，
勝前福德。」

尊重正敎分第十二

「復次，須菩提，隨說是經乃至四句偈
等，當知此處，一切世間、天人、阿修
羅，皆應供養，如佛塔廟；何況有人盡
能受持讀誦。須菩提，當知是人，成就
最上第一希有之法。若是經典所在之
處，即爲有佛、若尊重弟子。」

如法受持分第十三

爾時須菩提白佛言：「世尊，當何名此
經？我等云何奉持？」佛告須菩提：
「是經名爲『金剛般若波羅蜜』，以是

名字，汝當奉持。所以者何？須菩提，佛說般若波羅蜜，即非般若波羅蜜，是名般若波羅蜜。須菩提，於意云何？如來有所說法不？」須菩提白佛言：「世尊，如來無所說。」「須菩提，於意云何？三千大千世界所有微塵，是為多不？」須菩提言：「甚多，世尊。」「須菩提，諸微塵，如來說非微塵，是名微塵。如來說世界非世界，是名世界。須菩提，於意云何？可以三十二相見如來不？」「不也，世尊。不可以三十二相得見如來。何以故？如來說三十二相，即是非相，是名三十二相。」「須菩提，若有善男子、善女人，以恒河沙等身命布施；若復有人，於此經中乃至受持四句偈等、為他人說，其福甚多。」

離相寂滅分第十四

爾時須菩提聞說是經，深解義趣，涕淚悲泣而白佛言：「希有世尊，佛說如是甚深經典，我從昔來所得慧眼，未曾得聞如是之經。世尊，若復有人得聞是經，信心清淨，即生實相，當知是人成就第一希有功德。世尊，是實相者，即是非相，是故如來說名實相。世尊，我今得聞如是經典，信解受持不足為難。若當來世後五百歲，其有眾生得聞是經，信解受持，是人即為第一希有。何以故？此人無我相、無人相、無眾生相、無壽者相。所以者何？我相即是非相，人相、眾生相、壽者相即是非相。何以故？離一切諸相，即名諸佛。」佛告須菩提：「如是如是。若復有人得聞是經，不驚、不怖、不畏，當知是人甚為希有。何以故？須菩提，如來說第一波羅蜜即非第一波羅蜜，是名第一波羅蜜。須菩提，忍辱波羅蜜，如來說非忍辱波羅蜜，是名忍辱波羅蜜。何以故？須菩提，如我昔為歌利王割截身體，我於爾時無我相、無人相、無眾生相、無壽者相。何以故？我於往昔節節支解時，若有我相、人相、眾生相、壽者相，應生瞋恨。須菩提。又念過去於五百世作忍辱仙人，於爾所世無我相、無人相、無眾生相、無壽者相。是故須菩提，菩薩應離一切相發阿耨多羅三藐三菩提心，不應住色生心，不應住聲、香、味、觸、法生心，應生無所住心；若心有住，即為非住。是故佛說菩薩心，不應住色布施。須菩提，菩薩為利益一切眾生故，應如是布施。如來說一切諸相即是非相，又說一切眾生即非眾生。須菩提，如來是真語者、實語者、如語者、不誑語者、不異語者。須菩提，如來所得法，此法無實無虛。須菩提，若菩薩心住於法而行布施，如人入闇，即無所見；若菩薩心不住法而行布施，如人有目，日光明照，見種種色。須菩提，當來之世，若有善男子、善女人，能於此經受持讀誦，即為如來以佛智慧悉知是人、悉見是人，皆得成就無量無邊功德。」

持經功德分第十五

「須菩提，若有善男子、善女人，初日分以恒河沙等身布施，中日分復以恒河沙等身布施，後日分亦以恒河沙等身布施，如是無量百千萬億劫以身布施；若復有人，聞此經典信心不逆，其福勝彼，何況書寫、受持讀誦、為人解說。須菩提，以要言之，是經有不可思議、不可稱量無邊功德；如來為發大乘者說，為發最上乘者說。若有人能受持讀誦、廣為人說，如來悉知是人、悉見是人，皆得成就不可量、不可稱、無有邊、不可思議功德。如是人等，即為荷擔如來阿耨多羅三藐三菩提。何以故？須菩提，若樂小法者，著我見、人見、眾生見、壽者見，即於此經不能聽受、讀誦、為人解說。須菩提，在在處處若有此經，一切世間、天人、阿修羅所應供養，當知此處即為是塔，皆應恭敬作禮圍繞、以諸華香而散其處。」

能淨業障分第十六

「復次，須菩提，若善男子、善女人，受持讀誦此經，若為人輕賤，是人先世罪業應墮惡道，以今世人輕賤故，先世罪業即為消滅，當得阿耨多羅三藐三菩提。須菩提，我念過去無量阿僧祇劫，於然燈佛前，得值八百四千萬億那由他諸佛，悉皆供養承事，無空過者。若復有人，於後末世能受持讀誦此經，所得功德，於我所供養諸佛功德，百分不及一，千萬億分、乃至算數譬喻所不能及。須菩提，若善男子、善女人，於後末世，有受持讀誦此經，所得功德，我若具說者，或有人聞，心即狂亂、狐疑不信。須菩提，當知是經義不可思議，果報亦不可思議。」

究竟無我分第十七

爾時須菩提白佛言：「世尊，善男子、善女人發阿耨多羅三藐三菩提心，云何應住？云何降伏其心？」佛告須菩提：「善男子、善女人發阿耨多羅三藐三菩提心者，當生如是心：我應滅度一切眾生；滅度一切眾生已，而無有一眾生實滅度者。何以故？須菩提，若菩薩有我相、人相、眾生相、壽者相，即非菩薩。所以者何？須菩提，實無有法發阿耨多羅三藐三菩提心者。須菩提，於意云何？如來於然燈佛所，有法得阿耨多羅三藐三菩提不？」「不也，世尊。如我解佛所說義，佛於然燈佛所，無有法得阿耨多羅三藐三菩提。」佛言：「如是如是。須菩提，實無有法如來得阿耨多羅三藐三菩提。須菩提，若有法如來得阿耨多羅三藐三菩提者，然燈佛即不與我授記：『汝於來世當得作佛，號釋迦牟尼。』以實無有法得阿耨多羅三藐三菩提，是故然燈佛與我授記，作是言：『汝於來世當得作佛，號釋迦牟尼。』何以故？如來者，即諸法如義。若有人言如來得阿耨多羅三藐三菩提。須菩提。實無有法佛得阿耨多羅三藐三菩提。須菩提，如來所得阿耨多羅三藐三菩提，於是中無實無虛，是故如來說一切法皆是佛法。須菩提，所言一切法者，即非一切法，是故名一切法。須菩提，譬如人身長大……」須菩提言：「世尊，如來說人身長大，即為非大身，是名大身。」「須菩提，菩薩亦如是。若作是言：『我當滅度無量眾生』，即不名菩薩。何以故？須菩提，實無有法名為菩薩，是故佛說一切法無我、無人、無眾生、無壽者。須菩提，若菩薩作是言：『我當莊嚴佛土』，是不名菩薩。何以故？如來說莊嚴佛土者，即非莊嚴，是名莊嚴。須菩提，若菩薩通達無我法者，如來說名眞是菩薩。」

一體同觀分第十八

「須菩提，於意云何？如來有肉眼不？」「如是，世尊，如來有肉眼。」

「須菩提，於意云何？如來有天眼不？」「如是，世尊，如來有天眼。」

「須菩提，於意云何？如來有慧眼不？」「如是，世尊，如來有慧眼。」

「須菩提，於意云何？如來有法眼不？」「如是，世尊，如來有法眼。」

「須菩提，於意云何？如來有佛眼不？」「如是，世尊，如來有佛眼。」

「須菩提，於意云何？如恒河中所有沙，佛說是沙不？」「如是，世尊，如來說是沙。」「須菩提，於意云何？如一恒河中所有沙，有如是沙等恒河。是諸恒河所有沙數佛世界，如是寧為多不？」「甚多，世尊。」佛告須菩提：「爾所國土中，所有眾生若干種心，如來悉知。何以故？如來說諸心皆為非心，是名為心。所以者何？須菩提，過去心不可得，現在心不可得，未來心不可得。」

法界通化分第十九

「須菩提，於意云何？若有人滿三千大千世界七寶以用布施，是人以是因緣，得福多不？」「如是，世尊。此人以是因緣得福甚多。」「須菩提，若福德有實，如來不說得福德多；以福德無故，如來說得福德多。」

離色離相分第二十

「須菩提，於意云何？佛可以具足色身見不？」「不也，世尊。如來不應以具足色身見。何以故？如來說具足色身，即非具足色身，是名具足色身。」「須菩提，於意云何？如來可以具足諸相見不？」「不也，世尊。如來不應以具足諸相見。何以故？如來說諸相具足，即非具足，是名諸相具足。」

非說所說分第二十一

「須菩提，汝勿謂如來作是念：『我當有所說法』；莫作是念。何以故？若人言：『如來有所說法』，即爲謗佛，不能解我所說故。須菩提，說法者，無法可說，是名說法。」

爾時慧命須菩提白佛言：「世尊，頗有眾生，於未來世聞說是法，生信心不？」佛言：「須菩提，彼非眾生，非不眾生。何以故？須菩提，眾生眾生者，如來說非眾生，是名眾生。」

無法可得分第二十二

須菩提白佛言：「世尊，佛得阿耨多羅三藐三菩提，爲無所得耶？」佛言：「如是如是。須菩提，我於阿耨多羅三藐三菩提，乃至無有少法可得，是名阿耨多羅三藐三菩提。」

淨心行善分第二十三

「復次，須菩提，是法平等，無有高下，是名阿耨多羅三藐三菩提。以無我、無人、無眾生、無壽者修一切善法，即得阿耨多羅三藐三菩提。須菩提，所言善法者，如來說即非善法，是名善法。」

福智無比分第二十四

「須菩提，若三千大千世界中所有諸須彌山王，如是等七寶聚，有人持用布施；若人以此般若波羅蜜經乃至四句偈等，受持讀誦，為他人說，於前福德百分不及一，百千萬億分、乃至算數譬喻所不能及。」

化無所化分第二十五

「須菩提，於意云何？汝等勿謂如來作

是念：『我當度眾生』；須菩提，莫作是念。何以故？實無有眾生如來度者。若有眾生如來度者，如來即有我、人、眾生、壽者。須菩提，如來說有我者，即非有我，而凡夫之人以為有我。須菩提，凡夫者，如來說即非凡夫，是名凡夫。」

法身非相分第二十六

「須菩提，於意云何？可以三十二相觀如來不？」須菩提言：「如是如是：以三十二相觀如來。」佛言：「須菩提，若以三十二相觀如來者，轉輪聖王即是如來。」須菩提白佛言：「世尊，如我解佛所說義，不應以三十二相觀如來。」爾時世尊而說偈言：

若以色見我　以音聲求我

是人行邪道　不能見如來

無斷無滅分第二十七

「須菩提，汝若作是念：『如來不以具足相故，得阿耨多羅三藐三菩提。』須菩提，莫作是念：『如來不以具足相故，得阿耨多羅三藐三菩提』。須菩提，汝若作是念，發阿耨多羅三藐三菩提心者，說諸法斷滅。莫作是念。何以故？發阿耨多羅三藐三菩提心者，於法不說斷滅相。」

不受不貪分第二十八

「須菩提，若菩薩以滿恒河沙等世界七寶，持用布施；若復有人，知一切法無我，得成於忍；此菩薩勝前菩薩所得功德。何以故？須菩提，以諸菩薩不受福德故。」須菩提白佛言：「世尊，云何菩薩不受福德？」「須菩提，菩薩所作福德，不應貪著，是故說不受福德。」

威儀寂靜分第二十九

「須菩提，若有人言：如來若來若去、若坐若臥。是人不解我所說義。何以故？如來者，無所從來，亦無所去，故名如來。」

一合理相分第三十

「須菩提，若善男子、善女人，以三千大千世界碎爲微塵。於意云何？是微塵眾，寧爲多不？」須菩提言：「甚多，世尊。何以故？若是微塵眾實有者，佛即不說是微塵眾。所以者何？佛說微塵

眾，即非微塵眾，是名微塵眾。世尊，
如來所說三千大千世界，即非世界，是
名世界。何以故？若世界實有者，即是
一合相。如來說一合相，即非一合相，
是名一合相。」「須菩提，一合相者，
即是不可說；但凡夫之人貪著其事。」

知見不生分第三十一

「須菩提，若人言：『佛說我見、人
見、眾生見、壽者見。』須菩提，於意
云何？是人解我所說義不？」「不也，
世尊；是人不解如來所說義。何以故？
世尊說我見、人見、眾生見、壽者見，
即非我見、人見、眾生見、壽者見，是
名我見、人見、眾生見、壽者見。」
「須菩提，發阿耨多羅三藐三菩提心

者，於一切法應如是知、如是見、如是信解，不生法相。須菩提，所言法相者，如來說即非法相，是名法相。」

應化非眞分第三十二

「須菩提，若有人以滿無量阿僧祇世界七寶，持用布施；若有善男子、善女人發菩提心者，持於此經乃至四句偈等，受持讀誦、爲人演說，其福勝彼。云何爲人演說？不取於相，如如不動。何以故？

一切有爲法　如夢幻泡影

如露亦如電　應作如是觀」

佛說是經已，長老須菩提，及諸比丘、比丘尼、優婆塞、優婆夷，一切世間、天人、阿修羅，聞佛所說，皆大歡喜，信受奉行。

　　　　　金剛般若波羅蜜經終

回向偈

願消三障諸煩惱

願得智慧眞明了

普願罪障悉消除

世世常行菩薩道

About the English Translator

The Venerable Cheng Kuan

(1947-)

Ordained Taiwanese Buddhist monk, Abbot, Dharma Master, Dharma translator, Buddhist Sutra Commentator, Tai-Chi Chuan teacher, University Fellow at TCU Graduate School, B.A. in English, National Taiwan Normal Univ.

Currently:

- Ordained 53rd Generation Acharya of Hsin-Gong Sect, Koyashan, Japan (1996-)
- Abbot of Mahavairocana Temple (Taipei, Taiwan)
- Abbot of Americana Buddhist Temple (Michigan, USA)
- President of Vairocana Publishing Co., Ltd. (Taipei, Taiwan)

Publications:

A. English Writings

- *The Sutra of Forty-two Chapters Divulged by the Buddha.* (佛說四十二章經.) A translation from Chinese into English. An English-Chinese Text Version. Vairocana Publ., Taipei, 2005.

- *The Diamond Prajna-Paramita Sutra.*（金剛般若波羅蜜經.）A translation from Chinese into English. An English-Chinese Text Version. Vairocana Publ., Taipei, 2005; 2nd Ed., 2007

- *The Dharmic Treasure Altar-Sutra of the Sixth Patriarch.*（六祖法寶壇經.）A translation from Chinese into English. Annotated Ed. Vairocana Publ., Taipei, 2005.

- *The Sweet Dews of Ch'an.*（禪之甘露.）Lectures on Ch'an meditation. 1st Ed., Torch of Wisdom Publ., Taipei, 1990; 2nd Ed., Vairocana Publ., Taipei, 1995; 3rd Rev. Ed., Vairocana Publ., Taipei, 2002; 4th Ed., 2005.

- *Three Contemplations toward Buddha Nature.*（佛性三參.）Lectures on Ch'an meditation. Vairocana Publ., Taipei, 2002.

- *Tapping the Inconceivable.*（入不思議處.）Lectures on Ch'an and Mahayana practice. Vairocana Publ. , Taipei, 2002.

B. Chinese Writings

- 美國心戰綱領.（*The Strategic Principles of the U.S. Psychological Warfare*, U.S. Department of Defence.）A Chinese translation from English. Ministry of R.O.C., 1974.

- 說服：行為科學實例分析.（*Persuation: How Opinions and Attitude Are Influenced and Changed.*）A Chinese translation from English. Buffalo Publ., Taipei, 1979.

- 楞伽經義貫.（*A Commentary on Lankavatara Sutra.*）1st Ed., Mahayana Vihara Publ., Taipei, 1990; 2nd Ed., Manjusri Lecture Hall, Kaohsiung, 1995; 3rd Ed.,.Vairocana Publ., Taipei, 2007.

- 三乘佛法指要. (*The Writings of Kalu Rinpoche.*) A Chinese translation from English. Mahayana Vihara Publ., Taipei, 1990.

- 心經系列. (*A Series of Commentaries on Heart Sutra.*) Vairocana Publ., Taipei, 1997; 2nd Ed., 2005.

- 北美化痕(1). (*The Metamorphic Vestiges in America: a Collection of Speeches on Buddhism.*) Vairocana Publ., Taipei, 2001.

- 北美化痕(2). (*The Metamorphic Vestiges in America: a Collection of Speeches on Buddhism.*) Vairocana Publ., Taipei, 2001.

- 大乘百法明門論今註. (*The Treatise on the Portal of Mahayanic Centi-dharmic Apprehension: a New Commentary.*) Vairocana Publ., Taipei, 2002.

- 佛教邏輯學——因明入正理論義貫. (*Logicism in Buddhism—A Commentary on The Tractate on the Right Truth through the Comprehension of Causality Logicism.*) Vairocana Publ., Taipei, 2002.

- 大佛頂首楞嚴經義貫. (*A Commentary on The Surangama Sutra.*) Vairocana Publ., Taipei, 2006.

- 唯識三十論頌義貫. (*A Commentary on The Thirty-Gatha Tractate on Sole-Cognizancism.*) Vairocana Publ., Taipei, 2007.

- 觀所緣緣論義貫. (*A Commentary on The Tractate upon the Contemplation on the Factors Adhered to.*) Vairocana Publ., Taipei, 2007.

Formerly:

- Lecturer for the Samgha students of Chao-Shan Temple, Keelung, Taiwan. (1993-96)
- Lecturer of Tse-Ming Buddhist Research Institute, Ten Thousand Buddhas Temple, Taichung, Taiwan. (1994-95)
- Guest Lecturer to Massachusetts Institute of Technology, Boston. (1988)
- Buddhist Canon Teacher and Tai-Chi Chuan Teacher, Chuang Yen Monastery, Carmel, New York. (1988-89)
- President and Teacher, Lanka Buddhist Association, Dallas, Texas. (1987-88)
- Sutra Translator, Institute of Advanced Studies of World Religions, Brookstone, New York.
- Three year's Buddhist Retreat (March,1984 - May,1987)
- Lecturer and Executive Secretary, Buddhist Association of Dallas, Texas. (1983-84)

◎ 英譯者簡介◎

釋成觀法師：

台北市人，民國三十六年（1947年）生／1988年7月於美國紐約莊嚴寺披剃。同年於台灣基隆海會寺受三壇大戒。

學 歷：

國立台灣師範大學英語系畢業／台大外文研究所肄業／美國德州克里斯汀大學（Texas Christian University）英研所研究員。

佛學經歷：

◆ 美國德州閉關三年（1984-87）
　俄亥俄州閉關半年（1990）
◆ 日本高野山眞言宗第五十三世傳法灌頂阿闍梨（1996- ）

現 任：

◆（台灣）「大毘盧寺」住持
◆（美國）「遍照寺」住持

著 作：

A.中文著作

◆ 觀所緣緣論義貫.毘盧出版社，2007.
◆ 唯識三十論頌義貫.毘盧出版社，2007.
◆ 大佛頂首楞嚴經義貫.毘盧出版社，2006.

◆ 大乘百法明門論今註.（白話註解大乘百法明門論.）毘盧出版社，2002.
◆ 佛教邏輯學——因明入正理論義貫.（白話註解因明入正理論.）毘盧出版社，2002.
◆ 北美化痕(1).（佛學開示論文集.）毘盧出版社，2001.
◆ 北美化痕(2).（佛學開示論文集.）毘盧出版社，2001.
◆ 心經系列.（三階段、次第闡示心經之深義.）毘盧出版社，1997初版；1998初版二刷；2003初版三刷；2005第二版.
◆ 毘盧小叢書：
 1.『三世心不可得』（專題小手冊.）毘盧出版社，1992.
 2.『禪法述要與心經奧義』（專題小手冊.）毘盧出版社，1993.
 3.『三皈依要義』（專題小手冊.）毘盧出版社，1995.
 4.『五戒與在家律學示要』（專題小手冊.）毘盧出版社，1995.
◆ 楞伽經義貫.（註解楞伽阿跋多羅寶經.）大乘精舍，1990初版；佛陀教育基金會，1994初版二刷；高雄文殊講堂，1995第二版；毘盧出版社，2007第三版.
◆ 三乘佛法指要——卡盧仁波切手稿.（藏密文集.）英文漢譯：大乘精舍『慈雲雜誌』，1990.
◆ 說服：行為科學實例分析.英文漢譯：水牛出版社，1979.
◆ 美國心戰綱領.　英文原著美國國防部出版，英文漢譯：中華民國國防部，1974.

B.英文著作

◆ *The Sutra of Forty-two Chapters Divulged by the Buddha.*（佛說四十二章經.） 英譯本，經文英漢合刊，毘盧出版社，2005.

◆ *The Diamond Prajna-Paramita Sutra.*（金剛般若波羅蜜經.） 英譯本，附英文腳註，毘盧出版社，2005初版；2007第二版.

◆ *The Dharmic Treasure Altar-Sutra of the Sixth Patriarch.*（六祖法寶壇經.） 英譯本，附英文腳註，毘盧出版社，2005.

◆ *The Sweet Dews of Ch'an.*（禪之甘露.） 英文版，英語禪坐班隨堂開示文集. 毘盧出版社，1995第二版，2002第三修訂版；2005第四版.

◆ *Three Contemplations toward Buddha Nature.*（佛性三參.） 英文版，英語禪坐班隨堂開示文集. 毘盧出版社，2002.

◆ *Tapping the Inconceivable.*（入不思議處.） 英文版，英語禪坐班隨堂開示文集. 毘盧出版社，2002.

曾 任：

◆ 基隆・照善寺「菩提專修班」講師(1993-96)
◆ 台中・萬佛寺「慈明佛學研究所」講師(1994-95)
◆ 紐約・美國佛教會「莊嚴寺、大覺寺」講師(1988-89)
◆ 台北・光仁中學(1976-77)、中山女高(1977-78)英文教師
◆ 「國防部光華電台」翻譯官(1973-75)

Two Western Renditions
of Sanskrit Compared

Old Rendition (Latinized)	New Rendition (Anglicized)	Chinese Translation
Abhidhyā	1. Avarice 2. Greed 3. Attachment	貪；貪欲
Abhijñā	Supernal Power	神通
Ācārya	1. Acharya 2. Acarya	阿闍梨
Ādarśa-jñāna	Great Round-mirror Noesis	大圓鏡智
Akaniṣṭha	1. Akanistha 2. The Topmost Matterful Heaven	阿迦尼吒天； 色究竟天
Akuśalā-karma	Vile Karma	惡業；不善業
Ālaya	Alaya	阿賴耶
Ālaya-vijñāna	1. Alaya Cognizance 2. the Eighth Cognizance	1. 阿賴耶識 2. 第八識
Amitābha	Amitabha	無量光
Amitābha Buddha	Amitabha Buddha	阿彌陀佛
Anāgāmin	Anagamin	阿那含
Anāgāmi-phala	1. Anagamihood 2. Consummation of Anagamihood	阿那含果

Old Rendition (Latinized)	New Rendition (Anglicized)	Chinese Translation
	3. the Fruition of Anagamihood	
Anāsrava	Imperviousness	無漏
Anātman; Nirātman	Egolessness	無我
Anātman-dharma	Dharma of Egolessness	無我法
Anavatapta	Lake Anavatapta	阿耨達池
Aṇḍaja-yoni	Egg-begotten	卵生
Aniketa	Un-residing	無住
Animitta	Appearancelessness	無相
Anitya	Impermanency	無常
Aṇu-raja(s)	Molecule(s)	微塵
Anuttara-samyak-sambodhi	1. Supreme Enlightenment 2. Supreme Bodhi 3. Supreme Right Equitable Enlightenment 4. Ultimate Enlightenment	阿耨多羅三藐三菩提； 無上菩提； 無上正等正覺
Araṇā-samādhi	Noncontention Samadhi	無諍三昧
Āraṇya	Aranya; serene	寂靜
Araṇya	Aranya; hermitage	阿蘭那；阿蘭若
Arhat	Arhat	阿羅漢
Arhat-phala	1. Arhathood	阿羅漢果

Old Rendition (Latinized)	New Rendition (Anglicized)	Chinese Translation
	2. Consummation of Arhathood 3. Fourth Consummation	
Arūpa-dhātu	the Immaterial Realm	無色界
Asaṃkhya	Asamkhya	阿僧祇
Asaṃskṛta	Non-implementation	無爲
Asaṃskṛta-dharma	Dharma of Non-implementation	無爲法
Āsrava	Perviousness	漏；煩惱
Asura	Asura	阿修羅
Asura-gati	Asura Realm	修羅道；修羅趣
Ātman	1. Ego 2. I; Me	我
Ātma-dṛṣṭi	Ego-view	我見
Aupapāduka-yoni	Transformation-begotten	化生
Avalokiteśvara	1. Kuan-Yin 2. Avalokiteshvara	觀音（菩薩）； 觀世音（菩薩）
Avidyā	1. Inanity 2. Ignorance	無明
Bahu-jana	Multibeings	群萌；群生；眾生
Bhadra kalpa	the Virtuous Kalpa	賢劫
Bhagavāṃ	1. the World-Venerated One 2. Bhagavam	世尊；薄伽梵

Old Rendition (Latinized)	New Rendition (Anglicized)	Chinese Translation
Bhāvanā	Practice	修習
Bhikṣu	Bhiksu	比丘
Bhikṣuṇī	Bhiksuni	比丘尼
Bhīṣma-garjita-svara-rāja	Wei-Yin-Wang Buddha	威音王（佛）
Bīja	Seed	種子
Bodhi	1. Bodhi 2. Enlightenment	菩提；覺
Bodhicitta	Bodhi-Heart	菩提心
Bodhidharma	Bodhidharma	菩提達磨；達磨
Bodhisattva	1. Pusa 2. Bodhisattva	菩薩 菩提薩埵
Bodhisattva-yāna	Pusa-Yana	菩薩乘（大乘）
Bodhivṛkṣa	Bodhi-tree	菩提樹
Buddha	Buddha	佛
Buddha-cakṣus	Buddhaic Eyes	佛眼
Buddha-dharma	1. Buddha-dharma 2. Buddhaic Dharma	佛法
Buddha-gotra	Buddha Nature	佛性；佛種性
Buddha-jñāna	Buddhaic Noesis	佛智
Buddha-mārga	Buddhaic Way	佛道
Buddha-phala	Buddhahood	佛果

Old Rendition (Latinized)	New Rendition (Anglicized)	Chinese Translation
Bhūta-tathatā	Veracious-Thusness	眞如
Cakra-varti-rājan	Wheel-revolving Anointed King	轉輪聖王；轉輪王
Cakṣur-vijñāna	1. Visual Cognizance 2. Cognizance of Eye	眼識
Catur-yoni	Four Nativities	四生
Catvāri ārya-satyāni	1. Four Sacred Truths 2. Four Holy Truths	四聖諦
Catvāri jñānāni	Quadruple Noeses	四智
Chanda	Desire	欲
Citta	1. Heart 2. Mind	心
Dāna	1. Bestowal 2. Donation	施；檀那
Dāna-pāramitā	Bestowal Paramita	施波羅蜜
Daśakuśala-karmāni	1. Ten Good Deeds 2. Ten Virtues	十善；十善業
Daśakuśala-karma-pathāni	1. Ten Evil Deeds 2. Ten Vile Deeds 3. Ten Vices	十惡；十惡業
Deva	1. Heaven, Celestial 2. Celestial Being; Celestial Deity	1. 天 2. 天人
Deva-gati	Celestial Realm	天道；天趣

Old Rendition (Latinized)	New Rendition (Anglicized)	Chinese Translation
Deva-loka	Heaven, Celestial	天
Dharma	Dharma	法
Dharma-bhāṇaka	Dharma-master	法師
Dharma-cakra	Dharmic Wheel	法輪
Dharma-cakṣus	Dharmic Eyes	法眼
Dharma-dhātu	Dharmic Sphere	法界
Dharma-kāya	Dharmic Corpus	法身
Dharma-lakṣaṇa	Dharmic Appearance	法相
Dharmarakṣa	Dharmaraksa	竺法蘭
Dharmatā	1. Reality 2. Appearance of Reality	實相
Dhātu	1. Realm 　　eg: Three Realms 2. Domain 　　eg: 18 Domains 3. Sphere 　　eg: Dharmic Sphere	界 　（三界） 　（十八界） 　（法界）
Dhyāna	1. Ch'an 2. Stasis 3. Zen	禪；禪那 定
Dīpaṃkara Buddha	Lamp-Lighting Buddha	然燈佛
Divya-cakṣus	Celestial Eyes	天眼
Dṛṣṭi; Darśana	1. View 2. Apprehension	見；見解

Old Rendition (Latinized)	New Rendition (Anglicized)	Chinese Translation
Duḥkha	Affliction	苦
Duścaritāni	Vile Deeds	惡行
Dvātrimśan mahā-puruṣa-lakṣaṇāni	1. Thirty-two Auspicious Physical Appearances 2. Thirty-two Auspicious Appearances 3. Thirty-two Auspicious Features 4. Thirty-two Appearances	三十二大丈夫相； 三十二大人相； 三十二相
Dveṣa	1. Aversion 2. Destation	瞋；瞋恚
Eka-lakṣaṇa	Uni-appearance	一相
Eka-lakṣaṇa-samādhi	Uni-appearance Samadhi	一相三昧
Eka-vyūha-samādhi	Uni-execution Samadhi	一行三昧
Gandha-kāma	1. Desire for Smell 2. Desire for Aroma	香欲
Gaṅgā	Ganges (River)	恆河
Gaṅgā-nadī-vāluka	Gangesful-sand	恆河沙
Garbha	Repertory; Treasure	藏；寶藏
Gāthā	Gatha; Verse	偈
Ghrāṇa-vijñāna	1. Nasal Cognizance 2. Cognizance of Nose	鼻識
Guṇa	1. Merit 2. Meritorious Virtue	功德；求那

Old Rendition (Latinized)	New Rendition (Anglicized)	Chinese Translation
Guṇa	Dust	塵
Harītakī	Haritaki	訶梨勒；訶子
Hīnayāna	1. Hinayana 2. Minor Vehicle	小乘
Icchantika	Icchantika	一闡提
Indriya	Root	根
Iryā-pathāḥ	Dignified Carriages	威儀
Jambū-dvīpa	Yen-fu-ti (World)	閻浮提；瞻部洲
Jarāyuja-yoni	Womb-begotten	胎生
Jāta, Jāti	1. Nascence (Birth) 2. Genesis	生
Jāti-maraṇa	1. Nascence and Demise 2. Birth and Death	生死
Jetavana	Jetavana Park	祇樹給孤獨園
Jihvā-vijñāna	1. Gustatory Cognizance 2. Cognizance of Tongue	舌識
Jīvita	Lifespan	壽命
Kali-rāja	King Kali	歌利王
Kalpa	Kalpa	劫；劫波
Kalyāṇamitra	1. Good Guru 2. Good Mentor	善知識

Old Rendition (Latinized)	New Rendition (Anglicized)	Chinese Translation
Kāma	Desire	欲；愛
Kāma-dhātu	the Desire Realm	欲界
Karma	Karma	業
Karmāvaraṇa	Karmic Impediment	業障
Karuṇā	Compassion	悲
Kaṣāya	Cassock	袈裟
Kasyāpa	Kasyapa	迦葉
Kaśyapamātaṅga	Kasyapamatanga	迦葉摩騰
Kāuṇḍinya	Kaundinya	憍陳如
Kāya	1. Body 2. Corpus	身
Kāya-lakṣaṇa	Physical Appearance	身相
Kāya-vijñāna	1. Corporal Cognizance 2. Cognizance of Body	身識
Kleśa	Annoyance	煩惱；惑
Kṛtyānuṣṭhāna-jñāna	Task-Accomplishing Noesis	成所作智
Kṣānti	Forbearance	忍；羼提
Kṣānti-pāramitā	Forbearance Paramita	忍波羅蜜
Kṣānti-vādi-ṛṣi	Forbearant Sage	忍辱仙人
Kula-duhitri, Kula-dhītā	virtuous woman	善女人

Old Rendition (Latinized)	New Rendition (Anglicized)	Chinese Translation
Kula-putra	virtuous man	善男子
Kumārajīva	Kumarajiva	鳩摩羅什
Kuśala	Virtue	善
Kuśalā dharmāḥ	Good Dharmas	善法
Kuśalā-karma	Good Karma	善業
Kuśala-mūla	1. Virtuous Root 2. Good Root	善根
Lakṣaṇa	1. Appearance 2. Feature	相
Laṅkāvatāra Sūtra	Lankavatara Sutra	楞伽經
Laukika	1. Worldly 2. mundane	世俗；凡俗
Lobha	1. Avarice 2. Attachment	貪；貪欲
Loka	the mundane World	世間
Loka-dhātu	World	世界
Lokottara	Ultra-mundane	出世間
Lokottara-jñāna	Ultra-mundane Wisdom	出世間智
Mahā	1. Maha 2. Grand; Great; Mega	大；摩訶
Mahā-kalpa	Mega Kalpa	大劫
Mahā-kāśyapa	Mahakasyapa	大迦葉
Mahā-parinirvāṇa	Supreme Grand Nirvana	佛滅；大般涅槃；無上大涅槃

Old Rendition (Latinized)	New Rendition (Anglicized)	Chinese Translation
Mahāsāhasra-lokadhātu	Mega-thousand Worlds	大千世界
Mahā-sattva	Mahasattva	摩訶薩埵；摩訶薩
Mahā-sthāma-prāpta	1. Puissance-Advent 2. Mahasthamaprapta	大勢至（菩薩）
Mahāyāna	1. Mahayana 2. Major Vehicle	大乘
Maitrī, Maitrya	Benevolence	慈
Maitreya	Maitreya	慈氏；彌勒（菩薩）
Mama-kāra	1. Mine 2. Ajunct of mine	我所
Māṃsa-cakṣus	Naked Eyes	肉眼
Manas	Manas	意；思量
Manas-vijñāna	1. Manas Cognizance 2. the Seventh Cognizance	1. 末那識 2. 第七識
Mano-vijñāna	1. Deliberational Cognizance 2. the Sixth Cognizance	1. 意識 2. 第六識
Mantrāyana	Shingon Sect	眞言宗
Manuṣya	1. Mankind 2. Human being	人
Manuṣya-gati	Humanity Realm	人道；人趣
Māra	Mara	魔

Old Rendition (Latinized)	New Rendition (Anglicized)	Chinese Translation
Maraṇa	1. Demise 2. Death	死
Mārga	1. Route; Way 2. Truthful Way	道
Moha	1. Inanity 2. Ignorance	癡；愚癡
Mṛgadāva	Mrgadava	鹿野苑
Mūḍha	1. Inanity 2. Ignorance	癡；愚癡
Muditā	Jubilance	喜
Naraka	1. Hell 2. Purgatory	地獄
Naraka-gati	1. Hell Realm 2. Purgatory Realm	地獄道；地獄趣
Nayuta	Nayuta	那由他
Nigha	Sinful Karma	罪業
Nirmāṇa-kāya	1. Metamorphosic Corpus 2. Transformational Incarnation 3. Avatar 4. Avataric Corpus	化身；應身
Nirodha	Surcease	滅（諦）
Nirodha-samāpatti	1. Extinctive Stasis 2. Annihilative Stasis	滅盡定

Old Rendition (Latinized)	New Rendition (Anglicized)	Chinese Translation
Nirupadhi-śeṣa-nirvāṇa	Unremnant Nirvana	無餘涅槃
Nirvāṇa	1. Serene Surcease 2. Serene Terminnation 3. Termination	滅度；涅槃；寂滅
Nitya; śāśvata	1. Permanency 2. Constancy	常
Pañcābhijñā	Five Supernal Powers	五通；五神通
Pañca kāmāḥ	Five Desires	五欲
Pañca veramaṇī	Five Precepts	五戒
Pañcaskandha	1. Penta-aggregates 2. Five Aggregates 3. Five Umbrages	五蘊；五陰
Pañca vijñānāni	the First Five Cognizances	前五識；五識
Pañcendriyāṇi	1. Five Virtuous Roots 2. Five Good Roots	五根；五善根
Pāramitā	1. Paramita 2. Deliverance	度；波羅蜜（多）
Pātra	Alms Bowl	鉢
Pātra-cīvara	Cassock and Alms Bowl	衣鉢
Phala	1. Fruition 2. Consummation	果
Piṇḍa-grāha	Uni-amalgamated Holism	一合相

Old Rendition (Latinized)	New Rendition (Anglicized)	Chinese Translation
Prajñā	1. Prajna 2. Noesis 3. Transcendental Wisdom	般若 智 智慧
Prājñā-cakṣus	1. Eye of Wisdom 2. Sagacious Eyes	慧眼
Prajñā-pāramitā	Wisdom Paramita	般若波羅蜜
Prajñendriya	Wisdom Root	慧根
Prakṛti	1. Essence 2. Quintessence 3. Nature 4. Attribute	性；自性
Prāp; Prāpta	Obtainment	得
Pratigha	1. Aversion 2. Destation	瞋
Pratyavekṣaṇā-jñāna	Wondrous-Discernment Noesis	妙觀察智
Pratyeka-Buddha	Causality-enlightenist	緣覺
Pratyeka-buddha-yāna	Causality-enlightenist Yana	緣覺乘
Pravrajyā	Renouncing the Worldly Home	出家
Preta	1. Starving Ghost 2. Starving Ghost-kind	餓鬼
Preta-gati	1. Starving Ghost Realm 2. Starving Ghost-hood	餓鬼道；餓鬼趣

Old Rendition (Latinized)	New Rendition (Anglicized)	Chinese Translation
Puṇya	1. Merit 2. Bliss 3. Well-being	福
Puṇya-kṣetra	Meritorious Field	福田
Puruṣa-damya-sārathi	the Taming Master	調御丈夫
Pūrva-nivāsānusmṛti-jñāna	Supernal Wisdom of Providence	宿命智
Rāga	1. Avarice 2. Attachment	貪；貪欲
Rāga, Dveṣa, Moha	Avarice, Aversion (or Detestation), Inanity	貪瞋癡
Rajas	Desire	欲
Rasa-kāma	1. Desire for Taste 2. Desire for Flavor	味欲
Ṛṣi	Sage	仙人
Rūpa	1. Matter 2. Form 3. Material	色
Rūpa-dhātu	1. Material Realm 2. Matterful Domain	色界
Rūpa-kāma	1. Desire for Forms 2. Desire for Matter	色欲
Rūpa-kāya	Physical Body	色身
Śabda-kāma	Desire for Sound	聲欲

Old Rendition (Latinized)	New Rendition (Anglicized)	Chinese Translation
Ṣaḍ abhijñā	Six Supernal Powers	六通；六神通
Saddharma-vipralopa	1. *fin de siècle* 2. later-age	末世；末法
Ṣaḍ-indriyāṇi	Six Roots	六根
Ṣaḍ-pāramitā	1. Six Paramitas 2. Six Deliverances	六波羅蜜；六度
Ṣaḍ-vijñāna	Six Cognizances	六識
Sakradāgāmin	Sakradagamin	斯陀含
Sakradāgāmi-phala	1. Sakradagamihood 2. Consummation of Sakradagamihood	斯陀含果
Śākyamuni	1. Sakyamuni 2. Shakyamuni	釋迦牟尼（佛）
Samādhi	1. Samadhi 2. Dhyanic Stasis 3. Stasis	1.三摩地；三昧 2.禪定 3.定
Samādhīndriya	1. Tranquility Root 2. Stasis Root	定根
Samatā-jñāna	Equitability Noesis	平等性智
Saṃbhoga-kāya	Retributional Corpus	報身
Saṃgha	Samgha	僧伽；僧
Saṃjñā	Conception	想
Saṃsāra	1. Transmigration 2. Reincarnation 3. Samsara	輪迴；生死

Old Rendition (Latinized)	New Rendition (Anglicized)	Chinese Translation
Saṃskāra	Kinesis	行（蘊）
Saṃskṛta	Implementation	有爲
Saṃskṛta-dharma	Dharma of Implementations	有爲法
Saṃsvedaja-yoni	Moisture-begotten	濕生
Samudaya	Assemblage	集（諦）
Sapta ratnāni	seven kinds of jewelries	七寶
Śāriputra	Sariputra	舍利弗、舍利子
Śarīra	Relics	舍利
Sarvajña	Ominiscient Wisdom	一切智
Śāstā Deva-manuṣyaṇaṃ	Guru for All Celestials and Terrestrials	天人師
Sattva	Multibeings	眾生；有情
Satya-vāda	Veracious Saying	實語
Śīla	Precept	戒；尸羅
Śīla-pāramitā	Precept Paramita	戒波羅蜜
Skandha	Aggregate	蘊
Smṛti	1. Deliberation 2. Ideation	念
Smṛtīndriya	Deliberation Root	念根
Soha	Soha	娑婆
Sopadhi-śeṣa-nirvāṇa	Remnant Nirvana	有餘涅槃

Old Rendition (Latinized)	New Rendition (Anglicized)	Chinese Translation
Spraṣṭavya-kāma	1. Tactile Desire 2. Desire for Touch	觸欲
Śraddhā	Belief; Faith	信
Śraddhendriya	Faith Root	信根
Sramāna	Sramana	沙門
Śrāmaṇera	Sramanera	沙彌
Śrāmaṇerikā	Sramanerika	沙彌尼
Śrāvaka	1. Auricularist 2. Sravaka	聲聞
Śrāvaka-yāna	Auricular Yana	聲聞乘
Śrāvastī	1. Sravasti 2. Shravasti	舍衛國
Srota-āpanna	1. Srota-apanna 2. First Fruitioner	須陀洹
Srota-āpanna-phala	1. Srota-apannahood 2. Consummation of Srota-apannahood	須陀洹果
Śrotra-vijñāna	1. Audio Cognizance 2. Cognizance of Ear	耳識
Stūpa	1. Stupa 2. Pagoda	塔；窣堵波
Subhūti	Subhuti	須菩提
Sukhāvatī	1. the Elysian World 2. the West Elysian World	極樂世界

Old Rendition (Latinized)	New Rendition (Anglicized)	Chinese Translation
Sumeru	Sumeru	須彌(山)
Śūnya	1. Vacuous 2. Empty 3. Sunya	空；虛；舜若
Śūnyatā	1. Vacuity 2. Sunyata	空性；舜若多
Sūtra	Sutra	經；修多羅
Svahbāva	1. Quintessence 2. Intrinsic Essence	自性
Tathā	Thusness	如
Tathāgata	1. Thus-Adventist 2. Tathagata 3. Ju-lai	如來
Tīrthaka	1. External Wayer 2. Externalist	外道
Tiryagyoni	Animal	畜生
Tiryagyoni-gati	Animal Realm	畜生道；畜生趣
Trayaḥ kāyāḥ	Triple Corpuses	三身
Trayo-dhvanaḥ	Three Times	三世；三際
Tri-loka	Three Realms	三界
Trīṇi-karmāṇi	Three Karmas	三業
Trīṇi piṭakāni	Tri-canon	三藏
Trīṇi yānāni	Tri-Yanas	三乘

Old Rendition (Latinized)	New Rendition (Anglicized)	Chinese Translation
Tri-ratna	Triple Gems	三寶
Tri-sāhasra-mahā-sāhasra-loka-dhātu	Three Thousand Mega-thousand Worlds	三千大千世界
Tri-śaraṇa-gamana	Three Refuges	三皈依
Uccheda	Nihilistic Extinction	斷滅
Uccheda-dṛṣṭi	View of Nihilistic Extinction	斷滅見
Uccheda-lakṣaṇa	Nihilistically Extinctive Appearances	斷滅相
Upāsaka	Upasaka	優婆塞；清信士
Upāsikā	Upasika	優婆夷；清信女
Upāya	1. Expedite Means 2. Dexterous Means; Dexterity	方便
Upekṣā	Abnegation	捨
Utpāda-nirodha	Genesis and Perishment	生滅
Uttara	Ultimate	究竟
Vaiśāli	Vaisali	毘舍離；吠舍釐
Vajra	Dimond	金剛；伐闍羅
Vedanā	1. Perception 2. Sensation	受
Vijñāna	1. Cognizance 2. Conciousness	識

Old Rendition (Latinized)	New Rendition (Anglicized)	Chinese Translation
Vikurvaṇa	1. Supernal Transformation 2. Supernal Metamorphosis	神變
Vimalakīrti	1. Vimalakirti 2. Purified-Appellation	維摩詰（菩薩）；淨名
Vimokṣa; Vimukti; Mukti	1. Liberation 2. Emancipation	解脫
Vipāka	1. Retribution 2. Retributional Desert	果報
Vipaśyanā	1. Contemplation 2. Visualization	觀；毘婆舍那
Vīrya	1. assiduity 2. sedulity 3. industry 4. diligence	精進；進
Vīrya-pāramitā	Assiduity Paramita	精進波羅蜜
Vīryendriya	1. Assiduity Root 2. Diligence Root	精進根
Vyākaraṇa	Prognosticative Ordination Conferral	授記；記別
Vyūha kalpa	Majestic Kalpa	莊嚴劫
Yāna	Yana	乘
Yojana	Yojana	由旬；踰繕那

Glossary

A

Absolute Beingness: the theory that Being, or certain Beings are considered as absolute, constant, and unchangeable forever, such as the "soul." This is the so-called "Constant View," which is a kind of Devious View that would hinder practice.

abstemious: able to abstain or refrain from, or be liberated from Desires (specif., the Five Desires: the Desires for Wealth, Sex, Fame, Food, and Sleep).

Adherence: When an Attachment grows so strong that it becomes a dogged Tenacity, it is called Adherence.

Advent: coming.

Afflictional Sea of Life and Death, the: Reincarnation is viewed as full of afflictions without end; hence it is likened to a Sea of Sufferings, huge and boundless and full of perils.

Aggregates, the: i.e., the Penta-aggregates; specifically, Matter, Sensation, Conception, Kinesis, and Cognizance. These five Aggregates altogether would constitute the body and mind of Multibeings.

All the Appearances are vain and delusive: a famous quotation from *The Diamond Sutra*.

All the Multibeings: i.e., all living beings.

all the Thinkings should be exterminated: such as some External Wayers or most Hinayanaists would do.

Alter-appearance: i.e., the Views about other persons individually (singular number) from the self-centered standpoint.

ambulate around: a formality of behavior to show high reverence to a great master.

ambulations: i.e., walking meditation, as one of the highest form of showing respect to elders or holy people.

an aberrant person: a person who wanders away from the Truthful Way, or, to be specific here, from his own Original Nature. And so this term denotes all commonplace people, or the Multitudes.

Anagamin: the Third Consummation of Hinayanaic Sainthood. The Third Fruitioner will no longer come back to this world to be reborn. Hence this will be his Final Lifetime in this world; and at the end of this life, he will be born in the Akanistha Heaven, the topmost heaven in the Matterful Domain, where he will realize Arhathood and attain Nirvana.

Animal: The characteristic of Animal-hood is Inanity (stupidity).

Anuttara-samyak-sambodhi Heart: Sanskrit, meaning the "Heart for the Supreme Right Equitable Enlightenment." "Heart," here means Aspiration. This phrase can also be abbreviated as: the Great Bodhi Heart.

Appearance-free Precepts of Three Refuges: The Three Refuges are also considered as a Precept. But the "precepts" here are not meant to be conceived sheerly by its external outlook; hence they are called "Appearance-free."

Appropriations or Repulsions: i.e., takings or rejections.

Aranyaic: from Sanskrit *"Aranya,"* meaning forest; hence, hermitage.

Arcane: esoteric, secret.

Arcanum, the: the secret precious thing.

Asamkhyas: innumerable, countless; said to be about trillions of trillions.

Asuras: a genre of Celestial Beings, who enjoy very good Well-beings; but they are highly belligerent due to jealousy and anger, and so they are constantly at war with other Celestial Beings on that account.

attain the Truthful Way: i.e., to be enlightened.

Auricularists: i.e., the Hinayanaists, who acquire the Buddha's instructions entirely through "Hearing" hence.

avoid bearing the same name as the Master's: In Chinese tradition, it is considered as improper and irreverent to have the same name as that of one's seniors, especially elder relatives or teachers.

B

bare one's right shoulder: an ancient etiquette in India showing high respect to elders or superiors.

become intermingled with: acquire perfect comprehension and is in complete unison with the Dharma.

Bestowal: Donation, as the first item of the Six Deliverances (Six Paramitas), it is one of the most important practices for a Pusa, or Mahayanaic Practitioners in general, for it signifies the will to benefit other people, the very central animus of Mahayanaic Altruism.

Bhiksu: an ordained Buddhist monk.

Bhiksuni: an ordained Buddhist nun.

Blazing House, the: i.e., the Three Domains, in which the Multi-beings are being burned by the fire of Five Lusts.

Bodhi: Sanskrit, Enlightenment.

Bodhi-Site: the place where one practices for the attainment of Bodhi (Enlightenment).

Bondage of Dharma, the: i.e., to be bound by Dharma, rather than get liberations by means of Dharma.

Buddhaic Terra, the: the enlightened state of the Buddha.

Buddha's Mental Insignia: a metaphor for the most significant part of Buddha's teachings; it is like the official Seal of a king which is used to mean offical approval, or the highest authority, hence.

C

Capacious-Equitable Sutras, the: i.e., Sutras of the Major Vehicle.

carnal lust: i.e., sexual desire.

Cassock: an ordained Buddhist priest's robe.

Causal Constituents: The Cause is the major and direct determinant; the Constituent is the minor, or subordinate one; hence, an indirect influence. Usually, Causes are internal determinants, and Constituents are external ones.

Cessation-Contemplation: two of the most important techniques in meditation. Cessation means to cease mental Annoyance so as to make it tranquil. Contemplation means after Cessation is attained, one can go a step further to pratice Visualization on the basis of the tranquility gained by Cessation.

Chicaneries: deceptions.

Ch'an-master Hsing-Hsi: Master Hsing-Hsi and Master Huai-Rang are the two most massive pillars under the House of the Sixth Patriarch's. Out of these two great Masters, the lineage of the Sixth Patriarch grew and flourished, and came to dominate the Higher Teaching of Buddhism throughout history in China until modern days.

Ch'an-master Huai-Rang: cf. footnote above this one.

Common Plebeians: ordinary unenlightened people.

confer a Royal Appellation : to give a name to someone or something officially by the authority of the King; it was considered as a great honor, and the Appellation was usually personally written down in calligraphy by the conferer himself on a signboard, signed and affixed with his personal or official seal. And this affair is deemed as a very culturally refined, sophisticated, and arstic matter by men of letters in bygone days.

Confrontational Manifestation of Serene Surcease, the: i.e., the Serene Surcease (Nirvana) manifests itself right in front of the practitioner.

constituted by antithetical counterparts: i.e., founded by two conflicting elements.

Consummate Attestation: i.e., ultimate fulfillment.

Consummation of Arhat Way, the: the Fourth Consummation of Hinayanaic Sainthood.

Contingency: external agent.

Corporeal Pusa: *Pusa*: the Chinese abbreviated version for the transliteration of the Sanskrit word "Bodhisattva," a person aspired for the pursuit of Bodhi for the sake of achieving Ultimate Enlightenment both for himself and all living beings. A **Corporeal Pusa** is a saint (Pusa) who has transcended life and death, and so when he passes away, oftentimes his physical body would not decompose (without using any chemical treatment at all). Such a saintly person is called a Corporeal Pusa.

cultivation: same as practice.

D

Da-Huei: Great Wisdom.

darkened domicile of Annoyances, the: i.e., the Mind, which is constantly darkened by all sorts of Annoyances.

Detriments: harms, i.e., the intention to do harm to or kill others.

Devious Sects, the: i.e., Sects with fallacious beliefs and opinions.

Deviousness: crookedness.

Dexterity: deft means.

Dexterous Means: good, deft, skillful methods in teaching and practicing, derived from great wisdom of Good Gurus.

Dharma: Sanskrit, meaning law, or doctrine, or teachings. It can also mean "thing" or "being" which could include everything and anything in the world or beyond the world, either animated or inanimated, physical or spiritual, tangible or intangible. But when used to denote Buddha's doctrines or teachings, it is usually capitalized; otherwise, it will be in lowercase letters.

dharma: This word with the first letter in lower case (dharma) stands for "all beings," or anything in existence; whereas "Dharma" with a capitalized first letter usually stands for Buddha Dharma, or Buddha's Doctrines.

Dharmas of Implementations: i.e., all the mundane things or beings, for the fact that they are the outcome and effect of all sorts of "workings" (implementations).

Dharmas of Non-implementation: i.e., the Ultramundane Dharmas, or the Dharmas that can lead to Ultimate Liberation. "Implementation" means all kinds of illusory employments or undertakings of the worldly people.

Dharmic Appearance: This refers to Attachment to the Buddhist Doctrines.

Dharmic Corpus, the: the "Body" that is purely constituted by Dharma, and it can be attained only through Enlightenment.

Dharmic Noumenon, the: i.e., the "main body" of Dharma.

Dharmic Portal: i.e., the approach or means to the Dharma, which serves as a gate, or entrance, to the Truthful Way or Enlightenment.

Dharmic Spheres, the: There are Ten Dharmic Spheres; i.e., the Dharmic Sphere of Buddha (Dharmic Sphere hereafter shortened as "D.S."), the D.S. of Pusa, the D.S. of the Auricularists, the D.S. of the Causality-enlightenists, the D.S. of Celestial Beings, the D.S. of Humans, the D.S. of Asuras, the D.S. of Starving Ghosts, the D.S. of Animals, and the D.S. of Purgatory.

Dhyanaic Sitting: i.e., sitting meditation.

Dhyanaic Stasis: same as Samadhi.

Dhyanaic Stasis for Liberation: i.e., Liberation gained through Samadhi (Dhyanaic Stasis).

Diamond: the hardest material in the world, symbolizing the Transcendental Wisdom that can break all the bad Karmas and impediments while the diamond itself will not break.

Diamond Sutra, The: one of the most important and popular Sutras in the Major Vehicle teaching (Mahayana).

dichotomized: separated into two opposing parts; eg., good and evil; right and wrong, etc.

disciple of doctrine explicator, a: i.e., a Buddhist scholar specialized in Buddhist Scripture exigesis, rather than a practicing Ch'an Master.

disparate Indoctrinations: i.e., different beliefs.

Disportive Samadhi: When one is so good at Samadhi that one could enjoy doing it and treat it like entertainment; in this case, the Samadhi to that individual is called Disportive Samadhi.

Doctrinal Supernality: a Supernal Power that manifests itself in the thorough understanding and comprehension of the Dharma, as well as the ability to expound its purports.

Domains, the: i.e., the Eighteen Domains, which consist of the Six Senses,the Six Dusts and the Six Cognizances.

Dual Appearances, the: i.e., the two extremes, or two conflicting forces which are different in outlooks as well.

Dual Consummations: This denotes both Merits and Wisdom of the Buddha have been consummately realized. This is also a Meritorious Epithet for the Buddha.

Dual-Yanaist: the Two Yanaists; i.e., the Auricularist and Causality-enlightenist.

dwell: same as "reside," a very crucial key word in *The Diamond Sutra*, as well as in all the Buddhist practice, especially in Ch'an (or Zen) Buddhism. It means the Attachment or Tenacity in possessing and holding onto something, especially in showing the indolence to "move on." This is exactly the sentiment that we would hold with respect to the "house" we dwell in (both the material house and the "corporeal house," i.e., the physical body), which we would cling steadfast to, grow attached to, and would not let go of easily, not even when the "lease" is expired.

E

Edification: teaching.

Edificational: of teaching.

edify: to teach by preaching or some other way.

Eighth Cognizance, the: i.e., the Alaya Cognizance. This is the most important and substantial body of all Cognizances. Out of this Cognizance all other Cognizances grow and develop.

Egg-begotten, Womb-begotten, Moisture-begotten, and Transformation-begotten, the: Collectively these are called the Four Nativities.

Ego-appearance: i.e., Egoistic Views.

Ego-appearance, Alter-appearance, Multibeing-appearance, and Lifespan-appearance: These are the so-called Quadruple Appearances, the fundamental Attachments which would stand in one's way to Wisdom, Nirvana, and Enlightenment.

emergence or submergence: i.e., the beginning or the conclusion.

Emergence: appearance, said of the Buddhas' or Pusas' coming to be born in this world.

Emperor Liang-Wu: 502-547 A.D.

Epiphanic Radiance: "Epiphany," denotes instant and inspirational Enlightenment. When such Enlightenment occurs, there would be radiance emitting out of the body and the mind; hence, Epiphanic Radiance.

Equitability Noesis: the Wisdom to discern that all Multibeings are ultimately equal.

Equitability: equalness.

Equitable Mind: i.e., the Mind to treat all Beings equally well.

Equity: i.e., Equality.

Ethereal Space, the: i.e., the sky.

Expedite Dexterity: convenient and helpful means, usually derived from Pusa's Impervious Wisdom.

Exterior Phenomena: all the things and beings outside of ourselves.

External Wayers: people of other beliefs, who seek outwardly for Truth.

F

fin de siècle: French, end of the century (or age), or the later-age.

First Five Cognizances, the: the Cognizances of Eye, Ear, Nose, Tongue, and Body.

First Purport, the: the highest Tenet of Buddha Dharma.

Five Contumacious Sins, the: These include Killing one's own father, Killing one's own mother, Killing an Arhat, Bleeding a Buddha in the attempt of killing Him, and effecting Dissension among Samgha (the Order). These are the most egregious sins in Buddhism, much more atrocious than the Four Vital Prohibitions.

Five Umbrages: same as the Penta-aggregates, for the Aggregates can "shroud" the Native Mind in total darkness, hence. (*Umbrage*, from Latin, meaning shadow.)

Forbearant Sage: a practitioner practicing on Forbearance, which is very close to the Greek stoicism in ignoring the physical and spiritual pains or sufferings.

Four Assemblages: the disciples of the Buddha, both sacerdotal (i.e., Bhiksu and Bhiksuni) and secular (i.e., Upasaka and Upasika), altogether they are called the Disciples of the Four Assemblages.

Four Diagonal Directions, the: i.e., Northeast, Southeast, Northwest, and Southwest.

Four Grand Vows: These are the general vows that all Pusas are supposed to make for the attainment of the Supreme Bodhi (Enlightenment).

Four Vital Prohibitions, the: i.e., Killing, Stealing, Inappropriate Sex, and Lying. The violation of these four Precepts will cost the perpetrator the loss of their Life of Wisdom, and the degeneration into Vile Realms in their future reincarnations; therefore these wrongdoings are called "vital."

Fruition: the consummated stage.

G

Gate of Deliberation, the: i.e., the Sixth Cognizance.

Gatha: Sanskrit. A verse, usually composed of a quatrain (a four-line stanza), but it can be more than four lines. In Sanskrit, the Gatha used to be rhymed, but it is mostly unrhymed in the Chinese versions.

generate Bodhi-Heart: to be aspired to quest and practice for the attainment of Bodhi.

go into Surcease: i.e., go into Nirvana. Nirvana, Sanskrit, termination, meaning the termination of all Annoyances and Transmigrations.

Good medicines are usually bitter to the taste: an old Chinese maxim.

Good Mentor: a popular courteous addressing formality in Buddhism, especially in the Ch'an tradition, used to show high respect to the person or people addressed.

Grand Bhiksus: Bhiksu, an ordained Buddhist monk. Grand Bhiksus, referring exclusively to Arhats, the Hinayanaist Saints of the highest status.

Grand Enterprise, the: i.e., the pursuit of the Supreme Bodhi.

Grand Stasis: i.e., the Constant Stasis, which is the Samadhi as fulfilled by the Buddha.

Great Round Mirror Noesis: After the purified transmutation, instead of remaining a storehouse for impure Karmas as it used to be, the Alaya will transform into the general body of Wisdom to effect the realization of the Supreme Bodhi.

H

Holy Emergence: i.e., the Buddha's coming to this world.

horns of rabbits: i.e., an imaginary thing, which is totally impossible and non-existent. This is a very famous metaphor used by the Buddha in the Sutras.

Huang-Mei: i.e., the Fifth Patriarch.

Huang-Mei's: a euphemism for the place of the Fifth Patriarch's Temple. "Master Huang-Mei" in the next paragraph is also a euphemistic usage which refers to the Fifth Patriarch himself indirectly as a way of expressing veneration.

I

Icchantica: an unbeliever; one whose Virtuous Roots and Buddha-seed are exterminated.

Immotivity: the state of unmovement; unmovableness; impregnability.

Imperial Dharma-master: a title conferred by the emperor to a Master, who then is deemed as the Master for the entire Kingdom.

Imperviousness: the antonym of Perviousness; i.e., the quality of being invulnerable to Annoyances and Vitiations. This is the fulfilled state of Saints and Buddhas.

Implementation: working; execution.

impregnable: unmoveable; undestroyable.

in congruence with: i.e., at one with, corresponding with, or in tune with.

in congruence with the contingencies: acting according to situations.

In the drinking of the water, none but the Drinker himself knows exactly how cold or warm the water is: This statement, originally from one of the Buddha's Sutra, has been made a household axiom in China by *The Altar Sutra*.

Inaction: doing nothing.

Inanity: ignorance, or stupidity.

Incipience: the beginning stage.

Incipientless: too long ago to determine a spot for its beginning to the effect that it seems to be without a beginning, hence; beginningless.

Inconstant Mind: The Mind is vagarious and whimsical, and it is apt to change from instant to instant, hence.

Indigenous Mind: i.e., inherent Mind, same as the Original Nature.

ineffably inconceivable: that which is beyond words and thoughts.

Innate Entity, the: i.e., the substantial entity of the Original Nature.

Innate Essence: one's own inherent Essence; i.e., Original Nature.

Instantaneous Doctrines, the: i.e., the teaching of the Ch'an Denomination.

Instanteous Integration: i.e., to be integrated with the Truthful Way instantly.

inter-substitution: one substitutes for another incessantly.

J

Ju-lai: the Chinese translation (or rendition) of the Sanskrit Tathagata, meaning: the Thus-Adventist (Thus-Comer).

K

Kalpa: Sanskrit, aeons of ages.

Kalpa's Fire, the: It is said in the Sutras that at the end of a Mega-Kalpa, there will be a sequence of three great catastrophes: fires, deluge, and wind.

Karma: Sanskrit; originally meaning "working," "doing," and "operation." In one word, anything done, either visible or invisible, is considered as a Karma; for instance, the mental working is called "Mental Karma."

Karmic: the adjective form of Karma.

Kinetic Implementation: the movement and transiency of all beings.

King of Dharma, the: i.e., Buddha. This signifies that all Multi-beings are Buddhas in essence.

Ksana: Sanskrit, a very short instant. There are 60 Ksanas in one snapping of the fingers, and 900 Nascences and Demises in one single Ksana.

Kuan-Yin: Sanskrit: *Avalokiteshvara* ; the most popular Pusa in Mahayana.

Kumarajiva: 344-413 A.D., a great translator of Buddhist Canon, whose translations have been extremely popular in the Mahayana countries.

L

Lankavatara Sutra, The: the most important Sutra in both

Ch'an and Sole-Cognizance Sects. Also this Sutra is acknowledgedly one of the most abstruse Sutras in the Buddhist Canon.

Last Cycle of five hundred years, the: According to the Sutras, there are five cycles of 500 years, totally 2500 years, during which time Buddhism flourishes and declines gradually.

Lateral View: i.e., Side View, or Extremist Views.

Life and Death: This implies reincarnations;   i.e., the source of afflictions.

Lifespan-appearance: i.e., the Attachment to life or longevity, as concerns oneself, others, or all Beings in general.

Lotus: a symbol for the power and state to keep pure and uncontaminated in the midst of Defiled Surroundings. The color "Red" symbolizes fire, light and vitality.

M

Majestic Kalpa, the: An enormously big chunk of time is called a "Mega Kalpa," which is given a proper name for the whole period. For instance, in the past, there was the Majestic Kalpa, during which time there were one thousand Buddhas manifesting themselves in this Universe and became Buddhas. At present, the Kalpa is called the Virtuous Kalpa, during which there are also one thousand Buddhas, among whom only four of them have emerged so far. The rest of the 996 Buddhas will come in the future successively, and the next Buddha to come after Shakyamuni will be Maitreya Buddha, who will be born here about 5,670,000,000 years from now, as clearly prophesized in the Sutras.

majestify: to embellish and make magnificently beautiful. To get to the outcome of Majestivication would of course entail all the preparational procedures, such as cleaning and removing all the impurities (bad Karmas) at the outset. And so metaphorically it comes to mean to make betterments or improvements for Multibeings by leading them to practice the Dharma, so as to increase their true Well-beings (the "embellishments" with Buddhaic Merits).

Major Imports, the: the essential meanings; the most important points in the Tenets, or doctrines.

Major Vehicle: i.e., the Vehicle of Mahayana, which can accommodate a great number of people (that is, benefiting numerous people), as opposed to Hinayana, which generally aims at Self-deliverance as the final goal, benefiting none other than the practitioner himself—once with his goal achieved, he would never come back again, leaving all the unenlightened beings to be on their own.

Mara: a demonic celestial being, who usually becomes jealous when he descries people practicing the Truthful Way, and so he would not hesitate to throw all kinds of impediments in their way.

Marine Water: This implies an area boundless and hard to traverse.

Master Bodhidharma: the First Patriarch of Ch'an Buddhism in China. He came to China from India.

Material or Immaterial Beings, the Conceiving or Nonconceiving Being, the Unconceiving or Non-unconceiving Beings, the: These are the Celestial Beings of various levels, that have attained various stages of Stasis (Samadhi) in their previous lives, and were born in those Heavens according to their level of achievements in Stasis as a Retributional Desert.

Matter: i.e., physical or tangible stuff.

Mental Quickenings: Mental Emergences; i.e., the arising, or occurrence of a mental activity or functioning..

Mental Supernality: a Supernal Power that manifests itself incredibly in the thorough understanding or knowledge of other people's mind or thinkings.

Mental Terra: *Terra*, ground. The Mind is viewed as ground or earth,   wherefrom everything grows.

Mental Toils: same as Annoyances.

Meritorious Field: denoting a location or a person, where Merits can be cultivated and grown, usually talking of good Bhiksus or Bhiksunis (Buddhist ordained monks or nuns), to whom when people make offerings, the donors can accumulate merits for themselves from the donations made.

Mind: In Buddhism, usually the word "Mind" does not mean the brains, nor does the word "Heart" mean the physical organ. Both Mind and Heart, being the same character in Chinese, signify the spiritual entity of a living being, which is considered as the Primal Mover of everything, either within or without. Hence the Mind is not only the thinker, motivator, commander, and designer, but also the "feeler," "recipient," and the "ultimate enjoyer" of everything done or achieved, be it good or bad, sad or glad, thick or thin, life or death—the Mind would be the "Final Reaper."

Minor Dharmas: i.e., the doctrines of Hinayana and other Worldly teachings, or Externalist doctrines (that is, the teachings of other religions).

Mis-dharmic Appearance: This denotes the theories and practices contrary to Buddha's Teachings, and as such they are both fallacious and misleading.

misgivings: doubts.

Motivities: things that are in movement.

Mount Sumeru: the highest mountain in this Soha-world.

Multibeing-appearance: i.e., the View about other people conceived collectively (plural number) from the subjective self-centered standpoint.

Multibeings: the Multitudes. Yet this term includes not just people (mankind), but also the Beings in five other Realms; viz., the Celestial, Asura, Starving Ghost, Purgatory and

Animals. Together with Humanity, they are called the Six
Realms which constitute the Realm of Transmigration or
Samsara (Reincarnation).

Mundanity: i.e., worldliness, which is subject to Transiency.

N

Zenith and Nadir, the: i.e., up and down (top and bottom).

Nagaic Stasis: *naga*, Sanskrit, dragon, deemed as a fierce and
powerful being; thus, Nagaic Stasis, an impregnable, or un-
movable Stasis (Samadhi).

**Naked Eyes, Celestial Eyes, Sagacious Eyes, and Dharmic
Eyes, Buddhaic Eyes**: These are the well-known Five
Eyes of the Buddha, which connote the idea that the Buddha
would never "abandon" any Multibeings of any status until
they have eventually reached the Ultimate Enlightenment.

Nascence and Demise: Birth and Death; this is for animated
beings. For inanimated beings, it is called Genesis and
Perishment.

Nascence-Demise: Births and Deaths; i.e., Transmigration, or
Samsara.

Native Essence: also called Original Nature.

Naturalistic Externalist: "Naturalist" signifies one who believes
that enlightenment would come of itself ("naturally"), without the need of any effort or practice. This is refuted by the
Buddha as a Devious View. An "Externalist" is one who
seeks outwardly, such as in an external god or any other
factor, for enlightenment. Both of these Devious Views
combined together would result in an even more faulty conviction called "the Naturalistic Externalist Views."

nayuta: Sanskrit: one million, or ten million.

Nescience: unbrightness; without light; Ignorance.

Nihilistic Nothingness: the philosophical theory that everything will dissolve into nothingness when a living being dies, with absolutely nothing remained. (There are ample exemplars of these in Greek philosophy, such as the Atomism, the Mechanism, and Sophism, to name but a few. In modern western philosophy, materialism, pragmatism, and logical pragmatism all propagate in the Nihilistic vein.) This is the so-called "Extinctive View," or the Nihilistic View, which is the exact opposite of the Constant View. This view is even more heinous than the Constant View, for if everything were to go into nothing (extinction), then why should any-one bother to practice? However, the Constant View has the same misleading power as the Extinctive View does: if everything (for instance, the Soul) would remain always the same, no matter how hard you try to improve yourself, you would not be able to get it altered or improved in terms of Purification, then why should you bother to practice? There-fore, these two views are the worst obstacles for a True-Way Cultivator, for they would preclude the necessity and effort for practices, and as such they must be avoided by all means at the outset.

Nil-Noeses: i.e., without Noesis (wisdom) at all.

no antithesis: nothing against it.

Noeses: the plural form of *Noesis*, which is the highest wisdom of Buddha and great Pusas.

Noesis: the highest Wisdom of Buddhas or high-status Pusas. This term originally came from Greek, was first used in Platonism to mean the highest kind of knowledge or knowl-edge of eternal forms or ideas, and later used in Husserl to denote something else. From now on, this term will be em-ployed to denote the Consummate Wisdom of Buddha or other Enlightened saints.

Nonappearance: i.e., transcending all Appearances.

Nondescript Vacuity, the: There are three Attributes for things: good, evil, and nondescript. "Nondescript" denotes the quality of things that is neither good nor evil. The Non-descript Vacuity, however, would cause Inanity (stupidity or ignorance) to arise and develop in people's mind.

Non-attachment: no avarice.

Non-deliberation: not thinking.

Non-guru Noesis: the highest wisdom which enables one to be self-enlightened on anything one learns without instructions from others. Usually this is the Wisdom of Buddha, or a great Pusa.

Non-nascence: "No birth"; nothing has actually come into being, for everything is just like a phenomenon viewed in a dream, with phantasmal appearance, but totally ungraspable; hence, all Phenomena are un-nascent.

Non-recollecting: not recalling or remembering.

Non-residing Dharmic Bestowal: a term from *The Diamond Sutra,* meaning to bestow Dharmas to people for their benefit, and yet refrain from being attached either to the people benefited or the Dharma bestowed. This is the thematic gist of *The Diamond Sutra.*

Noumenal Entity: the fundamental "body."

Noumenon: the substantial body.

O

official Initiation for monks: a ritual or ceremony for people to become an ordained monk officially.

One Sole Entity: a unitary whole.

One Truthfulness: This implies the Original Nature , for it is the one and the only that is truthful, hence.

Original Visage: This is a very well-known term in Ch'an Buddhism, which stands for the Original Nature , or Buddha Nature.

Originality: i.e., the Original Nature.

P

Paramita: Sanskrit, "to the Other Shore." This means metaphorically that by means of Buddha's Transcendental Wisdom, all people (or beings) can traverse the River of Annoyances and Afflictions to "the Other Shore" of Nirvana or Enlightenment.

Patriarch Prajnatara of the West: the 27th Patriarch of Ch'an Denomination, the one preceding Patriarch Bodhidharma. West: i.e., India.

Penta-aggregates, the: i.e., the Five Aggregates: Matter, Sensation, Conception, Implementation (Kinesis), and Cognizance. Each of these is an aggregation of its own constituents.

Penuriousness: extreme stinginess.

Peril: danger.

Perviousness: Pervious originally means leaking, or penetrable; thus here Perviousness signifies the quality of being vulnerable to Annoyances and Vitiations (corruption). This is the state of ordinary Multibeings.

Plebeian: a Commonplace person; implying one who is not a Ch'an practitioner.

Plebeians, the: commonplace worldly people.

Portal: approach of practice, or the gate of Enlightenment.

Posthumous Epithet: an honorable name conferred to a person with high renown, merit, or contributions, after his death. This conferral is usually done by authorities, such as the emperor, or the royal authorities.

Practicing Outlooks: i.e., the way that practices are done.

Practitioner: a name for lay people who live in the temple to practice.

Prajna: Sanskrit: Transcendental Wisdom taught by the Buddha which can cure the Three Venoms (Avarice, Detestation, and Inanity), so as to attain the Supreme Enlightenment. This

Wisdom is totally different from the worldly intelligence or
cleverness which can do nothing about reducing bad Karmas or the Three Venoms. Prajna is also an Ultra-mundane
Wisdom, as opposed to the Mundane Wisdom (Worldly
Wisdom).

Prajnaic: adjective form of *Prajna*, Sanskrit, meaning Transcendental Wisdom.

Prajnaic Samadhi: i.e., the Stasis (Samadhi) realized through
Prajna (Transcendental Wisdom).

Precept, Stasis, and Wisdom: These are the Three Sacred
Learnings.

Priestly Scepter: a stick conferred to a monk at the official ordination.

Procreations and Perishments: i.e., Births and Deaths, or *Samsara* (Transmigration).

profound Dharmic Sphere: i.e., the consummate State (or
Sphere) fulfilled by Enlightenment.

Progenitors: i.e., the earliest Patriarchs.

Progenitor Buddha: the earliest Buddha.

Prognosticative Ordination: a Buddha's solemn and formal
prophesy and promise to someone about his candidacy for
the attainment of Buddhahood in the future, usually with
the details as to the date, the Appellation of the Buddha,
his family, his important disciples, and the duration of his
Dharmas.

Proper Sensation: another name for Samadhi;   for in Samadhi,
no Sensation whatsoever is seized or attached to, such a
state is called the Proper Sensation.

Prophetic Intimation: a prophesy rendered in an enigmatic or
hinting way.

Propriety: correctness.

Pseudonyms: In reality, all names are artificial; and so in the name per se there is actually no substantiality to be acquired. Although a name is used to stand for an entity of a thing or a being, yet the name is still not the entity itself; at best, it can only be utilized to denote or direct us toward the entity in question.

Puissant-Advent: Sanskrit: *Mahashamaprapta*. The name of a Pusa (Bodhisattva), who, with Kuan-Yin, constitutes the Dual-flanking Saints of Amitabha Buddha. Together they are called the Triple Holy Ones of the West Elysian World.

pulpit: In Buddhism, the lecturer is supposed to sit in meditation posture rather than stand on the platform, which is the practice of secular or worldly speakers. But nowadays many Buddhist lecturers stand while speaking, which is a great mistake, as well as 'Mis-dharmic,' which means that it is at odds with the teaching of Buddha Dharma.

Purely One Straightforward Mindedness: the uncrooked, undevious mind.

Purified Appellation: i.e., *Vimalakirti*, a Pusa in the manifestation of a lay practitioners.

Purified Belief: i.e., unadulterated faith, which is not contaminated by skepticism, self-interest, or other unnamed motives.

Pusa Mahasattvas: i.e., great *Bodhisattvas*. *Maha* means great in Sanskrit.

Pusa: the Chinese version for the Sanskrit *Bodhisattva*, meaning: one who seeks the fulfillment of Bodhi, or Enlightenment; next in rank to Buddha among all practitioners.

put to rout: i.e., be expelled, or done without.

Q

Quadruple Appearances, the: an important Doctrine as divulged by the Buddha in many Sutras, such as *The Diamond Sutra*; they are: the Ego-appearance, the Alter-appearance, the Multibeing-appearance, and the Lifespan-appearance. Please refer to the text of *The Diamond Sutra*.

Quintessence of Bodhi: Quintessence, the purest essence. *Bodhi*, Sanskrit, meaning enlightenment.

Quintessence of Constancy, the: The Mind of the Original Nature is not subject to Inconstancy or Transiency, and it is free from all Vitiations as well, hence.

R

Realization: same as Enlightenment.

Reciprocal Causality: the inter-relationship between Causes and Effects.

renounce the Worldly Home: i.e., to become a monk.

Repertory of Orthodox Dharmic Eye: another term for "the Supreme Dharma."

reside according to how he is instructed, to: i.e., to practice and live one's life by following the Buddha's teachings.

reveal itself with unchanged vividness: It is always as good as new. This is to depict the true state of the Original Nature.

reverse the Illumination back to yourself: another very significant concept and method in Ch'an Buddhism meditation.

Right Dharma, the: i.e., the orthodox Dharma.

Righteous advices are mostly displeasing to the ear: an old Chinese maxim.

S

Sacerdotal: i.e., priests, or monks and nuns collectively.

Sacred Status: the fulfilled holy state of either a Pusa or Buddha.

Sacred Truths, the: i.e., the Four Sacred Truths of Minor Vehicle.

Sagacious Eye: i.e., the Eye of Wisdom.

Sagacious Life, the: This is the meritorious Epithet that Subhuti had earned due to his outstanding wisdom.

Sagacity: the wisdom of Saints and Sages, or Pusas, which is of lower scale compared with the Buddha's Noesis.

Sakradagamin: the Second Consummation of Hinayanaic Sainthood. A Second Fruitioner will be able to attain Nirvana after one lifetime in the heaven and one rebirth (reincarnation) in this world.

Samgha: Sanskrit, meaning the Buddhist Order, or a group of ordained monks and nuns collectively. Although the word Samgha in its origin may mean an Assemgbly of either clerical or lay pelple, yet it has been traditionally used to refer to a group of priests exclusively; hence, it would be very inappropriate for a group of lay Buddhists to call themselves "a Samgha," which would involve a transgression of the Precepts; viz., "professing oneselves as ordained priests without really being so."

Sariputra: one of the Buddha's Ten Great Disciples, famous for his Wisdom.

Seminal Noesis: the seed of wisdom; the wisdom that is the origin, or genetic source of all wisdoms. This refers to the wisdom of Buddhas, Pusas, and other Saints.

Senses, the: i.e., the five senses.

Sentient-kind: same as Multibeings.

Sentiments: emotions.

Serene Surcease: i.e., Nirvana, the abolition of all Afflictions. This is the most used version of the Chinese translation of the Sanskirt term *Nirvana*.

Seventh Cognizance, the: i.e., the Manas Cognizance, which is the basis of Egotism.

Shingon Sect: the Esoteric Teaching of Buddha, originally transmitted from India to China in Tang Dynasty, and then from China to Japan; hence this sect is the Right Esoteric Dharma in Buddha's Orthodox Teachings.

sit and watch the Mind so as to contemplate on its Quietude: such as most Taoists usually would do.

Six Cognizances: This consists of Visual Cognizance, Audio Cognizance, Nasal Cognizance, Gustatory Cognizance, Corporal (or Tactile) Cognizance, and Deliberational Cognizance. The Cognizances as a whole would be the Mind; the individual Cognizances are the Mind's various functionings.

Six Dusts: Color (Matter), Sound, Smell, Taste (Flavor), Tactile, and Dharma. For these can make the Mind dusty, hence.

Six Gates: same as the Six Senses: Eye, Ear, Nose, Tongue, Body, and Ideation.

Six Heavens of Desires, the: In the Heavenly Realm of Desire, there are Six levels of Heavens, and because the Celestial Beings in each of these levels enjoy very exquisite things of desire, much more so than that which is enjoyed by Terrestrial Beings(Worldly Beings); therefore, they are called the Six Heavens of Desires.

Sixth Cognizance, the: i.e., the Deliberational Cognizance.

Sixth Patriarch, the: i.e., the Sixth Patriarch of Ch'an Buddhism, or Ch'an Denomination (Ch'an, also called Zen, in the Japanese pronunciation of the same Chinese character, 禪.)

Sixty-two Views: Devious Views as a whole, for all told, there are sixty-two of them, hence.

Sramana: Sanskrit, a priest or monk. Sramana originaly means: one who practices diligently to get rid of the Three Venoms.

Sramanera: Sanskrit, a male Buddhist novice for priesthood.

Srota-apanna: Sanskrit, meaning "entering into Stream (of sainthood)." This is the first Fruition (or Consummation) of Hinayanaic Sainthood. The First Fruitioner can attain Arhathood and realize Nirvana after seven reincarnations (seven rebirths) in this world.

stagnated: i.e., obstructed or detained.

Stasis: The Sanskrit word for Stasis is *Dhyana*. *Dhyana* in Buddhism is achieved by means of meditation, which is done in sitting in the lotus posture (cross-legged), and through the special techniques of Contemplation (i.e., Vipasyana) taught by the Buddha. And its outcome can bring miraculous transformations both in the mind and the body.

Strayed: same as aberrant.

stupa: Sanskrit, a Buddhist pagoda, usually built in honor of a Buddha, Pusa, or high priest, in which their physical relics are kept both for commemoration and for prosterity to worship.

Subhuti: one of the Ten Great Disciples of the Buddha, renowned for his Wisdom in Comprehending the tenet of Vacuity.

subject to undergoing Samsara pointlessly: i.e., to suffer Samsara (or Transmigration) for nothing.

submerge yourself under Vacuity and become vegetated in Quietude: Such is the way of practice as most Minor Vehiclists tend to do; yet this way of practice is not recommended for Mahayana practictioners.

Substantiality, the: meaning the substance of the Mind, or the Native Mind.

Sumeru: Sanskrit, the highest mountain of this Soha World; here it symbolizes something hard to overcome.

Supreme Bodhi, the: i.e., the attainment of Buddhahood.

Supreme Grand Nirvana, the: the Nirvana as fulfilled by the Buddha.

Sutra: Sanskrit, Buddhist Holy Scripture.

Sutra of Grand Nirvana, The: a very important Sutra in Mahayana, expounding Buddha Nature, which is the ultimate source for the Supreme Grand Nirvana; i.e., the Buddhaic Nirvana, as distinguished from that of an Arhat.

Sutra of Purified Appellation, The: also named: *The Vimalakirti*

Sutra. The Sanskrit word *"Vimalakirti,"* as the protagonist or main speaker in this Sutra, means "purified appellation. He was a renowned lay Buddhist at Buddha's time. And this Sutra is also a very important Scripture in the Ch'an Lineage.

T

take Cognizance of: recognize.

Taming Master, the Guru for all Celestials and Terrestials, and the Buddha, the: These are three of the Ten Meritorious Epithets (titles) of the Buddha, which he won by his Merits.

Task-Accomplishing Noesis: the Wisdom that can carry out and bring into fulfillment of whatever is to be done. This is one of the Four Buddhaic Noeses.

Terminational Liberation: i.e., Nirvana.

Thirty-two Auspicious Physical Features: The Buddha, through ages and ages of practice, has acquired some very extraordinary physical Features, which are deemed as very auspicious, such as the sign on the breast, the ear-lobes, which extend as long as to the shoulders, etc. These Features are auspicious in that if one contemplates in meditation on any of them, one could accumulate very good merits in the Karma through such meditation.

Three Genuses, the: They are the Umbrages (or Aggregates), the Domains, and the Ingresses.

Three Impediments, the: the Karmic Impediments, Annoyant Impediments, and Retributional Impediments.

Three Karmas, the: the Physical Karma, the Oral Karma, and the Mental Karma.

Three Temporal Confines: i.e., the Three Times: the past, present, and future.

three thousand Dignified Carriages and eighty thousand Meticulous Demeanors: These refer to the rules of conduct for all ordained monks and nuns as decreed in all the Sutras of Precept by the Buddha.

Three Thousand Mega-thousand Worlds: i.e. a Buddhaic World, consisting of 100 billion solar systems. This would include: a) One Mini-thousand Cosmoses (i.e., a universe, consisting of 1000 solar systems); b) One Medi-thousand Cosmoses (consisting of 1000 Mini-thousand Cosmoses); c) One Mega-thousand Cosmoses (consisting of 1000 Medi-thousand Cosmoses). Hence, altogether they are called the Three Thousand Mega-thousand Worlds. ("World," meaning one solar system, not just the planet Earth.)

Three Times, the: i.e., the past, the present and the future.

Three Venoms, the: Avarice, Aversion, and Inanity (or Attachment, Detestation, and Ignorance).

Three Vices, the: Killing, Stealing and Adultery.

Thus-Adventist, the: Sanskrit: *Tathagata*. This is also one of the Ten Holy Epithets of the Buddha, meaning: the "Thus-Comer," or "Thus-come one," in some other translations. *"Thus,"* in the manner of the Truthful Way as well as of the Sentient-kind's Karmic Occasions. *"Comer,"* one (the Buddha) who manifests Himself in this afflicted world (*Advent*) to salvage the Multibeings, due to compassion.

Thus-thusness: i.e., the Veracious Thusness; same as the Original Nature. Thusness" signifies the consummate state of Buddha-hood. The use of the doublet in this term refers to both the internal and the external state of "thusness." Specifically, it means the perfect Enlightenment that both the *interior* (mind-body-speech) and the *exterior* (the surrounding external objects and living Beings) are in the quality of "thusness"; hence this is called the state of "Thus-thusness." (Cf. Chinese *Ju-Ju*, 如如.)

Tien-Tai: an important Denomination (Sect) in Chinese Buddhism; specialized in the study and promulgation of *The Lotus Sutra.*

transcend Plebeianhood: to overcome the state of Commonplaceness.

transmute: to transform or alter the quality completely.

Triple Karmas, the: same as the Three Karmas; i.e., the Physical Karma, the Oral Karma, and the Mental Karma.

Tri-Yanaists, the: the Pusa, Auricularist, and the Causality-enlightenist. The Pusa is of the Major Yana, the Causality-enlightenist is of the Medium Yana, and the Auricularist is of the Minor Yana.

Truthful Way, the: i.e., the way for Bodhi, or Enlightenment.

Tsao-Hsi: i.e., the Sixth Patriarch of Ch'an Buddhism, a euphimistic usage.

Twelve Genres of Sutras, the: the twelve kinds of styles of the Sutras by which the Buddha preached the doctrines.

U

Ultraism: extremism; the extremist's view.

unbegotten and unperishing: i.e., beyond Life and Death, transcending Reincarnation, or Transmigration. "Unbegotten and unperishing" is one of the most important Tenets or Concepts in Ch'an Buddhism.

Unbiased Learning of Stasis-Wisdom: i.e., to practice Stasis and Wisdom equally and evenly.

Noncontention Samadhi: the state of Stasis (tranquility) plus Prajna (Transcendental Wisdom). "Noncontention" means the state free from all annoyances and strifes (Contentions). Hence the Noncontention Samadhi is a highly prestigious form of Samadhi, attained only by very few great Disciples of the Buddha's.

Undichotomized: not divided into two conflicting parts; not dualized.

Undichotomized Dharma: i.e., the Ultimate Truth is supposed to be only One, and so it cannot be dichotomized.

undivorced: not separated from.

un-exiting and un-entering: uncoming and unleaving.

Uni-amalgamated Holism: In the Worldly people's eye, everything appears to be "an indivisible whole," although they are, as a matter of fact, put together (or assembled) by various discrete parts. This is especially true of beings with life, either animated (animals) or inanimated (plants). Ordinary people tend to view things of life as an "Organism," which they would presume to be an indivisible whole, and therefore would consider them as not subject to changes. And so these people are, as it were, justified in being attached to their own Ego, so as to stay as what they are, to be complacent with themselves, to enjoy and pamper their own status quo, and finally to refuse to improve or cultivate themselves in whatever way. As a result, they would become so attached to their own image (Ego-appearance) that they would generally detest, reject, or repel anything disparate from their Ego, such as other individuals (Alter), or other people collectively (Multibeings). And this is the fundamental cause for all the *delusive differentiations* in life, whereby all the worries, and eventually afflictions and pains in life come into being. These problems all derive from the conviction of the specious *Holism*, which is, to a major degree, responsible for most kinds of conceptual ignorance.

Uni-appearance Samadhi: uni-appearance, or "one-appearance," said of the unified outlooks during the cultivation of this Samadhi.

Uni-implementational Samadhi: a form of very high-status

Samadhi as divulged in *The Lotus Sutra* and other Sutras.

Uni-performance Samadhi: Samadhi attained by executing it in one single posture, such as the Constantly Walking Samadhi, the Constantly Standing Samadhi, the Constantly Sitting Samadhi, the Half-Sitting half-walking Samadhi, etc.

Universal Reverence: i.e., the respect for all beings, which could only be the result of the total Abolition of one's Ego.

unparalleled: i.e., unrivaled; without a match; supreme.

Unremnancy: i.e., the *Unremnant Nirvana*, in which no more Transiencies are left.

Unremnant Nirvana: the Nirvana as attained by Buddhas and Pusas, which is consummate, leaving no Impurified Habitudes of Annoyances, as opposed to the Remnant Nirvana of Arhats or general Hinayanaists.

unstagnant: untenacious and undogged.

Untrammeled Supernal Power: unrestricted supernatural power.

unvitiated and unattached: uncontaminated and uncorrupted.

Upasaka: Sanskrit, a Buddhist male lay practitioner who has officially taken the Five-Precept Vows in a ceremony presided by a qualified Bhiksu in a shrine hall.

Upaseka: Sanskrit, a Buddhist female lay practitioner who has officially taken the Five-Precept Vows in a ceremony presided by a qualified Bhiksu in a shrine hall.

upright: i.e., without deceptions and crookedness of any kind.

V

vacuate the Mind, to: to try to make the mind "empty" by not thinking of anything at all. This method is erroneous, and so should be done away with. Similarly, in recent days, there are some people who claim to have "vacuated their body," i.e., to make their body seem to "disappear" or "invisible" either totally or partially (such as becoming invisible in the hands or the feet or the torso). These "Contemplative Visions" are virtually hallucinations resulted from bad Karmas as well as Devious Views. They are apparently illusive and erroneous, and are dangerously misleading, too. In the final analysis, these delusive visions result from a very strong attachment to the physical appearance on the one hand, and from the faulty comprehension about the Dharma on the other hand. If one fails to become aware of these being delusive phenomena, they could develop into Maraic Phenomena, which would frequently render the practitioner to fall into some uncontrollable habitual hallucinations (such as illusive auditions, internal dialogues either at the ear or within the body, etc.), and worst of all, they would eventually drive one into derangement. Therefore, all Truthful Ch'an cultivators would be better off to keep himself/herself away from these extremely pernicious "promising-looking" *Visions*, or "Attainment-like" *Pseudo-transmutations.*

Vacuity: Sanskrit: *Sunyata*, meaning emptiness, a highly specialized term in Buddhism. Specifically, it signifies that nothing has an independent, "Ego-nature" or "Ego-appearance" of its own, for everything is constituted from various amalgamated parts, and these parts are inter-dependent and inter-related to form an "apparent whole," which does not stay intact even for a very short duration, and which is subject to the law of Inconstancy; hence it undergoes changes, even from instant to instant. Therefore, its ultimate Ego-nature is ungraspable and unobtainable. For the Ego-appearances of things are thus unobtainable, it is then said that the Ego-nature of all Beings is Vacuous. And so the term Vacuity is used to denote such state of being.

Vajra: Sanskrit; the original meaning is diamond, which is the hardest mineral in the world; hence it stands for hardness, steadfastness and impregnability.

Venoms: i.e., the Three Venoms: Avarice, Aversion and Inanity; for these three are most poisonous to our mind, hence.

Veracious Corpus: i.e., the Relical Body of a Saint or Pusa. When the Sixth Patriarch of Ch'an Sect passed away in sitting meditation posture, his entire body became "one whole relic," which, miraculously, would never deteriorate or decompose. This, in Chinese Buddhism, is called "the Corporeal Pusa," which is a compassionate manifestation of Buddhas or Pusas to evince to the worldly people the Truthfulness of their Teachings by their Personal Bodily Examples (which through practice has transcended decomposition and vitiation, due to its ultimate purification). And this also manifests the Inconceivability of the Dharmas.

Veracious: truthful.

Veracious Thusness: The Essence of this is the same as Original Nature.

Vile Realms, the: i.e., the Three Vile Realms: Purgatory, Starving Ghost, and Animal.

Vimalakirti: a Pusa in Buddha's time, who manifested as a lay practitioner. The reason why Sariputra was reprimanded by Virmalakirti was because Sariputra might be "submerging into Vacuity and becoming stagnant in Serenity." That is the so-called "Nirvanaic Pleasure," or "Dhyanaic Pleasure," which is adverse to the practice of the Pusa, who is not supposed to indulge himself in such personal pleasures.

Virtuous Kalpa, the: see note of "the Majestic Kalpa" above.

Virtuous Roots: that which can effect all merits to live and grow. There are Five Virtuous Roots: Faith Root, Diligence Root, Deliberation Root, Stasis Root, and Wisdom Root. They are called "roots," because all the Virtues are engendered out of these fundamental Good Roots, just as the life of a plant depends on its roots for nourishment and stability.

Votaries and Votaresses: i.e., monks and nuns.

Votive Dharma: the Dharma that is oriented on Vows.

W

Waves of the Sea: Waves are usaually caused by wind, symbolizing Annoyances caused by External Phenomena.

Wei-Yin-Wang Buddha: a Buddha in the antediluvian age.

well divulged in the Commencement, Middle, and Denouement: said of the Buddha's Sutra, which is perfectly delivered in any portion.

West Universe, the: i.e., the West Cosmos, or the Pure Land of Amitabha Buddha in the West.

Wheel-revolving Anointed King: In Hindu folklore, a mighty emperor who ruled a vast kingdom with beneficence, rather than by force, and who was loved and respected universally—such a great sovereign or benign ruler was called a Wheel-revolving Anointed King.

'Wherever one's habitat is, one should remain in constant Composed Felicity': a quotation cited from *The Lotus Sutra*.

White-ox Carriage, the: a symbole for Mahayana.

Wind or the Banner, the: a well-known forensic theme in Ch'an.

Wisdom: i.e., Prajna, or Transcendental Wisdom, as opposed to Worldly Wisdom.

with Dignified Carriage: i.e., according to Buddhist etiquette.

without a back and without a face: i.e., there are no pros and cons, propriety and impropriety, right and wrong with it.

without a head and without a tail: i.e., without a beginning or ending.

without a name and without any appellation: i.e., beyond all indications and descriptions; ineffable.

without raising a single Notion: without conceiving any thought.

Wondrous-Discernment Noesis: the Wisdom that can discern and distinguish all sophisticated facets of all Dharmas. This is also one of the Four Buddhaic Noeses.

'Words are of no use': This has been one of the grossest misunderstanding about Ch'an Buddhism. There is a very celebrated painting in a book on Japanese Culture, with the caption of "Master Huei Neng Ripping off Books of Sutras." How could that be true? To say the least of the fact that the Patriarch himself got enlightened on *The Diamond Sutra*, which he encourages everyone to read right from the outset, let alone the Master's own words here denouncing the devious views about the abolition of Words in Buddhist cultivation. It should be called to the attention of all Ch'an students that the aforesaid painting is not only an ignorant imaginary product based on the painter's own ignorance and misunderstanding about Zen, but also a calumny on our Patricarch, which is derived from some inane evil views of later-day "Wild-Ch'anists," who due to bad Karma and lack of wisdom practiced Ch'an in the wrong way, and thereby misled the world by their views of foolish arrogant fervent iconoclastic-complex: A genuine Ch'an cultivator would take pity on their petty destructive misdeeds, and defend the Right Dharma.

World-Venerated One, the: Sanskrit: *Bhagavam*. One of the Ten Holy Epithets of the Buddha, meaning: one who is venerated by all the worlds, or worshipped universally.

Y

Yen-fu-ti World: an area of this Buddha-World; i.e., this solar system.

INDEX

A

Abstemious/abstemious 19, 20
Acharya 3
Advent 5
Afflictions 3
Akanistha Heaven 18
Alms 4
Alter 7, 12, 13, 19, 29, 30, 31, 35, 39,
    43, 53, 59, 60
Alter-appearance 7, 13, 29, 30, 31,
    39
Alterlessness 51
Alter-view 60
Altruism 8
amalgamated 58, 59
Anagamihood 18
Anagamin 18
Analogue 14
Animal(s) 6, 37
Annoyances 3, 7, 11
Anointed 54
ante meridiem 33
Anuttara-samyak-sambodhi 5, 6, 14,
    16, 31, 35, 37, 39, 40, 41, 42, 50,
    51, 55, 56, 60
anywhere 57
Appearance(s)/appearance(s) 7, 8, 9,
    10, 11, 12, 13, 26, 27, 28, 29, 30,
    31, 39, 48, 49, 56, 59, 61, 62
Appellation 41
Aranya 20
Aranyaic 20

Arhat(s) 4, 7, 19, 20
Arhat Way 19
Arhathood 17, 18, 19, 20
Asamkhya(s) 37, 61
Aspiration 5
assimilate(-s, -ing)/Assimilation 16,
    23, 24, 27, 28, 29, 34, 35, 36,
    37, 38, 52, 61, 63
Asura(s) 6, 24, 36, 63
Attachment(s) 7, 8, 13
attaining 40
Auspicious 26, 27, 53, 54
Avarice 3

B

bared his right shoulder 4
Begging Rule 4
Being(s) 6, 7, 13, 24, 36, 62, 63
Belief 11, 12, 28, 29, 34
berserk 38
Bestowal(s)/bestowals 8, 9, 31, 32,
    34, 47, 51, 61
bestowing 8
Bhagavam 4
Bhiksu(s) 4, 14, 62, 63
Bhiksunis 63
Bliss 47
Blissful Virtues 8, 9, 15, 16, 23, 27,
    47, 56, 57
Bodhi 5, 61
Bodhi-Heart 61
Bodhisattva(s) 5, 6

M

Maha 6
Mahasattvas 6, 21
Mahayana 34
Mahayanaic 8
Mahayanaic Altruism 8
Mahayanaic Practitioners 8
Majestification/majestification 21, 43
Majestify/majestify(ing) 21, 43
Major-vehicle 34
Mal-residing 31
Master 3
Material 7
Matter 8, 21, 31, 54
Matterful Domain 18
meager 16, 23, 24, 27, 52, 61
Medi-thousand 15
Mega-thousand 15, 23, 25, 47, 52, 58
meridiem 33, 34
Meritorious Virtues 28, 33, 34, 35, 38, 56
Merits 21
Mind(s) 5, 39, 46
Mini-thousand 15
Minor Dharmas 35
Mis-dharmas 13, 14
Mis-dharmic 13
Moisture-begotten 6
Molecules/molecules 25, 26, 58
Mount(s) 22, 51
Multibeing(s)/multibeings 5, 6, 7, 11, 12, 13, 19, 21, 29, 30, 31, 32, 36, 35, 39, 42, 43, 45, 46, 49, 50, 52, 53, 59, 60

Multibeing-appearance 7, 13, 29, 30, 31, 39
Multibeinglessness 51
Multibeings-Multibeings 50
Multibeing-view 60
Multitudes 6
mundane 3, 15
Mundane Wisdom 3
mutilated 30

N

Nadir 9
Naked Eyes 43, 44, 45
Nativities 7
Nayuta/nayuta 37
neither 57
Nihilistic 55
Nihilistically 56
Nirvana 3, 7, 11, 17, 18, 39
nirvanize 42
No Returning 18
Noesis 33
Non-alter-view 60
Non-appearance(s) 11, 27, 29, 31
Non-Buddhaic 16
Non-common-plebeians 53
Nonconceiving 7
Noncontention 19
Noncontention Samadhi 19
non-dharmic 15
Non-dharmic-appearances 61
Non-ego 53
Non-ego-view 60
Non-forbearance-paramita 30
Non-good-dharmas 51
Non-implementation 15

Donors for Publishing
The Diamond Prajna-Paramita Sutra
助印「英譯金剛經」(第二版)功德名錄

台幣部分：(NT$)

NT$3940元： 慧笙、慧洵
NT$2000元： 賴劉淑媛、黃必明、陳美玲、黃獎善
NT$1000元： 柯蔡宗親會、定藏、何孔明、何美玉、李心尹、李
　　　　　　 直宸、蘇子文
NT$800元： 定本
NT$600元： 徐鶴展
NT$500元： 慧現、蔡洪麵、蔡知音、拾獲、慧參、慧玄、慧
　　　　　　 彥、圓康、圓誼、吳素蘭、吳淑貞、慧堅、圓進、
　　　　　　 定一、定道、定地、圓持
NT$400元： 林志偉、林余霞、陳寶珠、慧善、慧香、慧呈
NT$200元： 定深、圓儀、邱銘鐘、鐘萬瓊、鐘白菊、陳瓊瑤、
　　　　　　 王李丹、慧恆、慧覺、詹馥慈、陳錦祥、慧任、圓
　　　　　　 穎、圓哲、鄭媛心、慧禮
NT$100元： 慧望、慧深、慧造、劉芷沅、劉春煌、慧暘、劉承
　　　　　　 鈞、定明、黃忠川、黃文隆、黃炳誠、黃仔婷、定敬
NT$40元： 　何漢根、何林鳳、吳榮裕、吳坤龍、何有騰、吳家
　　　　　　 豪、吳駿勝、吳佳玲

美金部份：(US$)

US$60： 圓蓮
US$50： 慧本
US$20： 圓靜、圓應、慧彰、慧顯、慧山、李尚嵐、曲桂梅、李
　　　　　 日明、劉雅俊、蘇賢武
US$10： 定詮、慧依、慧解、蔣鳳儀、蔣憲中、吳依蓮、圓道、

　　　　圓德、圓純、圓盛、阮瓊仙、Rich 黃、Tiffany 黃、圓
　　　　芝、慧光、慧儀、慧端、慧明、慧藏、圓節、陳衍隆、
　　　　陳遠碩、陳慧玲、簡朱英、陳張多、圓善、慧錦、圓
　　　　慧、圓恖、圓忠、圓孝、圓仁、慧綱、慧紀、圓逸、黃
　　　　遙凡、慧尚、圓眞、圓至、慧瑩、慧淳、圓持、何曉嵐
US$6：　圓現、圓義、侯馨鈞、侯國川、黃阿娥、林何玉惠
US$4：　圓殊、Lavern D. Loomis、圓恆、圓毅、圓立、圓勤、
　　　　圓瑾、圓定
US$2：　慧徹

「毘盧印經會」基本會員名單

釋成觀、釋成如、潘美鳳、黃忠川、黃炳誠、黃文隆、黃仔
婷、陳秀眞、潘麗碧、林秀英、張淑鈴、李錫昌、李陳紫、李
淑媛、李宗憲、陳慧眞、李淑瑩、李怡欣、李啓揚、張大政、
王月英、張金員、游鄭碧蓮、黃瑞豐、鐘玉燕、蕭惠玲、曾玉
娘、吳蕭幼、王元傑、宮林玉蘭、李琪華、王文君、宮貴英、
宮桂華、林煜榮、李英彰、蔡秀卿、詹淑涵、劉秀瑛、陳秀
芳、吳龍海、蘇金滿、謝幸貞

「遍照印經會」基本會員名單

釋成觀、釋成如、吳曉、簡慶惠、陳衍隆、陳遠碩、陳慧玲、
邵豐吉、邵陳世玉、陳永瑞、邵千純、陳雯萱、陳怡仲、陳怡
寧、唐永念、陳國輝、吳秀芬、葉潔薇、黃振、邵俊雄、李應
華、林斌、梁美好、蘇清江、李念眞、唐永良、詹朱界宗、
Lavern Dean Loomis、詹雅如、梁美容、嚴愛民、何林鈞、李
宗勳、許碧鳳、Joseph Charles Swartz、蘇才輔、蘇才鈞、張心
華、李郁芬、李安怡

國家圖書館出版品預行編目資料

金剛般若波羅蜜經　=　The Diamond Prajna-Paramita
Sutra　/　釋成觀英譯．　--第二版．　--臺北市：
毘盧，2007〔民96〕
　　面；　公分，　--（法海譯叢；2）
英漢合訂本
ISBN 957-9373-20-5（平裝）

1.般若部

221.44　　　　　　　　　　　　　　94013446

回向偈

願以此功德
莊嚴佛淨土
上報四重恩
下濟三塗苦
若有見聞者
悉發菩提心
盡於未來際
修行無上道

金剛般若波羅蜜經
The Diamond Prajna-Paramita Sutra

英譯者：釋成觀法師
發行者：大毘盧寺(台灣)・遍照寺(美國)
出版者：毘盧出版社
登記處：行政院新聞局局版台業字第5259號
贈送處：(1)台灣・大毘盧寺
　　　　台北市11691文山區福興路4巷6弄15號
　　　　Tel：(02)2934-7281・Fax：(02)2930-1919
　　　　郵政劃撥：15126341釋成觀
　　　　(2)美國・遍照寺Americana Buddhist Temple
　　　　10515 N. Latson Rd., Howell, MI 48855,USA
　　　　Tel: (517)545-7559・Fax: (517)545-7558
承印者：田園城市文化事業有限公司
版　次：佛曆2551年(2007年2月)春節第二版敬印一千冊
國際書碼：ISBN 957-9373-20-5

南無護法韋馱尊天菩薩

Namo Wei-to Pusa, the Honorable Celestial Guardian of Mahayana